THE 100 SHOW

THE NINETEENTH ANNUAL OF
THE AMERICAN CENTER FOR DESIGN

American Center for Design
325 West Huron
Chicago, Illinois 60610

PRESIDENT   Chris Conley
CHAIR   Meredith Davis
BOARD OF DIRECTORS Andrew Blauvelt
                   Stephen Cassell
                   Shelley Evenson
                   Peter Girardi
                   Bill Hill
                   Margo Johnson
                   Katherine McCoy
                   Frederick Murrell
                   Chris Myers
                   Aura Oslapas
                   Tucker Viemeister
                   Susan Yelavich

PUBLISHED BY   RotoVision SA
                   Rue du Bugnon 7 CH-1299
                   Crans-Près-Céligny, Switzerland

                   RotoVision SA, Sales Office
                   Sheridan House,
                   112-116a Western Road
                   Hove, East Sussex, BN3 1DD, UK

DISTRIBUTED IN THE US   Butterworth Heinemann
AND CANADA BY   225 Wildwood Avenue
                        Woburn, MA 01801-2041, USA

ISBN   0-8230-6365-9
PRODUCTION   ProVision Pte. Ltd.
AND PRINTING BY   34 Wilkie Road
                   Singapore, 228054

CONTENTS

FOREWORD

KATHERINE McCOY*

It is my pleasure, on behalf of the board of directors, to present this volume of winners from the American Center for Design 19th 100 Show competition. The 100 Show holds a special place among graphic design competitions. It identifies not only current trends in visual communication, but also the edges of design practice where individuals explore ideas not yet seen in the mainstream of practice. Projects included in this competition represent the work of established firms for well-recognized clients, designers devoting their personal time to important work for nonprofits, and students exploring new frontiers through previously unpublished work. It is the goal of this competition to surface new thinking about the solution of communication problems and to anticipate the "next" ideas to shape our field.

The format for the judging of the 100 Show also sets it apart. Unlike most design competitions in which winners are determined by juror consensus, the 100 Show is "curated." A competition chair selects three jurors after careful consideration of what they bring to contemporary discourse on design. Each juror picks his/her own show against individually determined criteria. The results are three points of view about design and interesting intersections of thought around works that attract the eye and mind of more than one juror. The essays by these jurors provide a context for their selections, as well as commentary on where we stand as a profession.

This book also documents important ideas in other fields. In keeping with the curated format, essays by leading designers and critics on new products and new media provide personal insights about what the future may hold. "Snapshots" of the year in review, these essays also serve as harbingers of things to come.

This year's competition was chaired by Michael Rock. The American Center for Design selected Michael for his versatility and his leadership in setting an agenda for design. A designer, educator, and author, Michael Rock has his finger on the pulse of design practice and criticism. Confirming the wisdom of this decision, Michael has assembled a diverse group of jurors whose abilities to critique and articulate thoughts about design are evident in the following pages.

We hope you enjoy the glimpse of the future that unfolds in this book.

*PRESIDENT, AMERICAN CENTER FOR DESIGN, BOARD OF DIRECTORS, 1994-1996

EVERY NOW AND THEN

MICHAEL ROCK, CHAIR, 19TH 100 SHOW

When is NOW? April 10, 1999, 2:35:37 PM. Downtown New York City, 45°, overcast. The Clash, *Guns of Brixton* (circa 1982) on the stereo. Writing with a 7-year old version of a 300-year old typeface on a 3-year old computer about an event that happened 2 years ago in another city.

Does design ever have a NOW? Can design ever be current? Is that the point of books like this, to capture a specific moment?

The NOW of design is a peculiar one. The forms of design – books, brochures, even web sites and film titles – tend toward the synchronic: they unify time and mask their own making. A book is published, it's about a subject, it bears a publication date. But when is the design finished? Is a design done when the electronic file is shipped? At the moment the print impression is made? The instant the final trim is trimmed? When a reader opens it? When it finally crumbles away to dust? Is the work in this catalog done?

This is the fourth complete introduction I have written for this book: which one is correct? The event that this catalog documents is now a memory. The work it celebrates is already historicized. Each introduction has fallen victim to the demands of being contemporary. The project itself, as it plowed on through the ACD's political and administrative turmoil, has outlived all our attempts to capture NOW.

Each time we dragged the increasingly archaic files out of the archive, we couldn't help re-thinking the design issues at hand. As the book lay dormant, we had changed. The way we think about design keeps changing. (I can see why Tschichold reverted to traditionalism late in life; modern is so exhausting.)

Our original intention was to make a pocket-sized book. To our dismay we learned that by law, all ACD 100 Show books must now be 9x12 inches. So we embedded our little book in a bigger one that frames *award-winning* design within a field of visual culture, the mundane examples counterpoint the stellar ones.

As we started collecting examples from the dirty world of common design, we realized that those examples were evidence of the NOW of this catalogue. The moment of making was mirrored by decisive devices: the daily newspaper, the dated memo, the postal meter stamp, the FedEx form, the computer log all chronicle a time-based process.

The time of this book, however, as it stretched from one year to the next, worked to defy the emphemerality of the framing device. Each moment blurred. The catalogue became a catalogue of out-dated images, multiplied past tenses. A string of THENS.

So rather than a catalogue of NOWs – which is always a fantasy – this is a catalogue that embraces THENs. It doesn't compare the winning entries to the great political images of the day the way the *Business as Usual* catalog did, (see essay by Somi Kim.) These are common objects. Most of the stuff here is part of the design of everyday life, the things you encounter in normal, informal settings: the record store, the book shop, the library, the bus shelter. So our comparisons are banal to banal: nothing more, nothing less.

It is the competition itself, of course, that is at the heart of the matter. At the start my role was simply to choose three judges and beg them to join me in Chicago. My goal was to find three eloquent writers who happened to be compelling designers/typographers that spanned an ideological spectrum. I am proud to report that Somi Kim, Abbott Miller, and Robin Kinross perfectly captured that agenda. I am indebted to them for giving so generously of their time and writing so thoughtfully.

The ACD 100 is known for, and even emblematic of, individualistic vision. Judges are compelled to curate collections. Consensus is shunned. I was, however, more interested in the cross-over selections than the individual choices. Where do our ideas of beauty and interest intersect? So the selections here represent a series of negotiations and overlaps. What do they mean? I leave that for you to figure out.

Now, for all you cultural studies scholars – twenty, thirty, fifty years from now – trying to decipher the design of the late nineties by scrutinizing primary sources like this one: Good luck. Looking around I get the sense that the community of designers is more unified than is often supposed. I get a whiff, now and then, of a little optimism. The ideological/generational battles that marked the beginning of the decade have, for the most part, faded. I am not sure who won, but that was THEN, this is NOW.

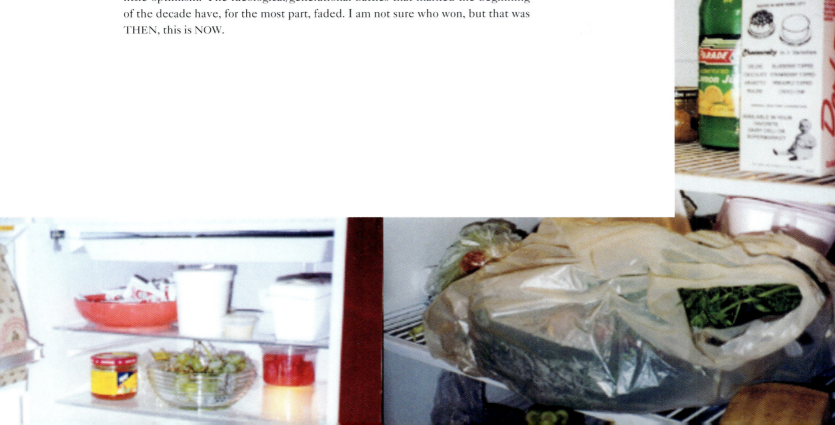

SELECTED BY   SOMI KIM   ROBIN KINROSS   J. ABBOTT MILLER

BAD RELIGION "THE GRAY RACE"

CD PACKAGING

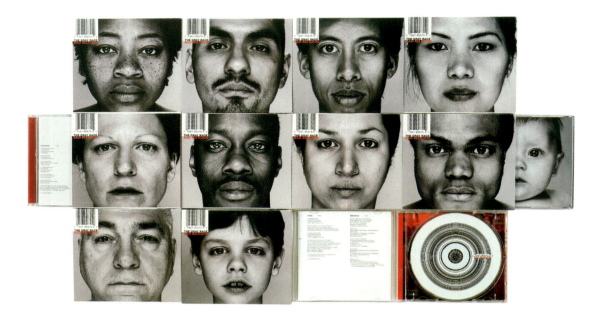

DESIGNERS Frank Garguilo and STAIN   DESIGN FIRM Atlantic Records

CREATIVE DIRECTORS Richard Bates   ART DIRECTOR Frank Garguilo   DESIGN ASSISTANCE Ryan McGuiness

PRINTER Ivy Hill   PHOTOGRAPHERS Richard Burbridge, band photo by Frank Ockenfels

BLUES, BOOGIE, AND BOP: THE 1940S MERCURY SESSION

BOOK COVER

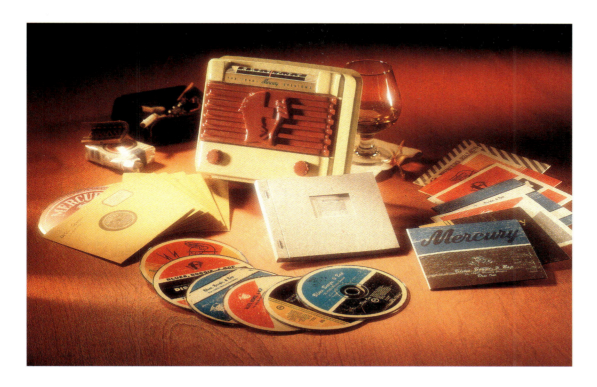

DESIGNER Giulio Turturro   DESIGN FIRM Verve Records   CREATIVE DIRECTORS Giulio Turturro, David Lau

CLIENT/PUBLISHER Verve Records   WRITERS Dan Morgenstern, Lorenzo Thomas   ILLUSTRATOR Giulio Turturro

PRINTER Enterprise Press   PAPER French Speckletone   PHOTOGRAPHER Various   TYPOGRAPHER Giulio Turturro

BOISE CASCADE OFFICE PRODUCTS 1995

ANNUAL REPORT

ENTRANT'S COMMENTS We were so impressed with the performance and history of this company, we wanted to put it right on the cover. What makes Boise so compelling is that this is its first annual report. We were also compelled by the monotony of its products. Being a commodity, office products are not what differentiates the company from the competition. It's what Boise did with them – its service, performance, customer satisfaction, etc. Therefore, our graphic concept was to use these common products in an unusual way, and, in so doing, demonstrate the remarkable performance of this company. We photographed the products simply and humbly so, by contrast, the performance statistics would be more impressive. The background colors were inspired by the simple colored papers offered by office products companies. The book was printed on uncoated paper to further support the honest, straighforward nature of the presentation and the company.

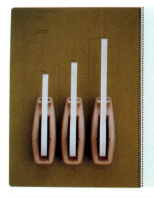

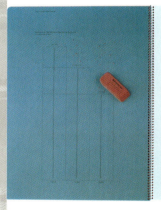

DESIGNERS Robert Petrick, Laura Ress   **DESIGN FIRM** Petrick Design

CREATIVE DIRECTOR Robert Petrick   **CLIENT/PUBLISHER** Boise Cascade Office Products   **WRITERS** Various

PRINTER The Hennegan Company   **PAPER** Mohawk Superfine Ultra White Smooth, Boise Cascade Ivory

PHOTOGRAPHER Chuck Shotwell   **TYPOGRAPHER** The Henderson Company

A BRIEF ON THE AGENCY (IN BRIEF)

BOOK

ENTRANT'S COMMENTS Coca-Cola asked us to create a document that explained how to brief an advertising agency. Our primary audience consisted of Coke's brand managers. Our secondary audience consisted of ourselves. We were inspired by children's primers. The book form suggests an object meant to endure. The simple presentation intends only to convey information. We used case binding with a heft and proportion that is inviting to hold. The red-and-white color scheme represents the company and seems consistent with the educational tone of the piece. The typeface – large, unadorned, easy to read – promotes the virtue of clear communication.

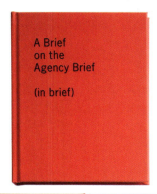 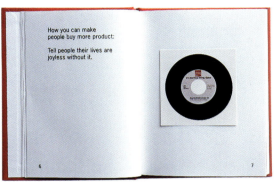

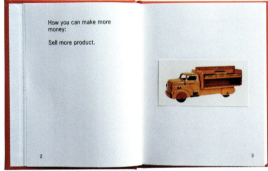 

DESIGNER Todd Waterbury   DESIGN FIRM Wieden & Kennedy   CREATIVE DIRECTOR Todd Waterbury, Peter Wegner   CLIENT/PUBLISHER The Coca-Cola Company   WRITERS Peter Wegner   PRINTER Schultz/Wack/Weir   PAPER Accent Opaque Vellum   PHOTOGRAPHERS Various   TYPOGRAPHER Todd Waterbury

BUILDING IN FRANCE, BUILDING IN IRON, BUILDING IN FERROCONCRETE

BOOK

ENTRANT'S COMMENTS Published in the book series, *Texts & Documents*, the design of the first English translation of Sigfried Giedion's 1928 architectural text follow the original design intent by Giedion as closely as possible. By paying close attention to the nuances of the original typography and by ensuring that pictures, captions, text, and footnotes appear in the same location in these pages as they did in the original, we successfully sustained Giedion's original vision, and culturally preserved a significant work.

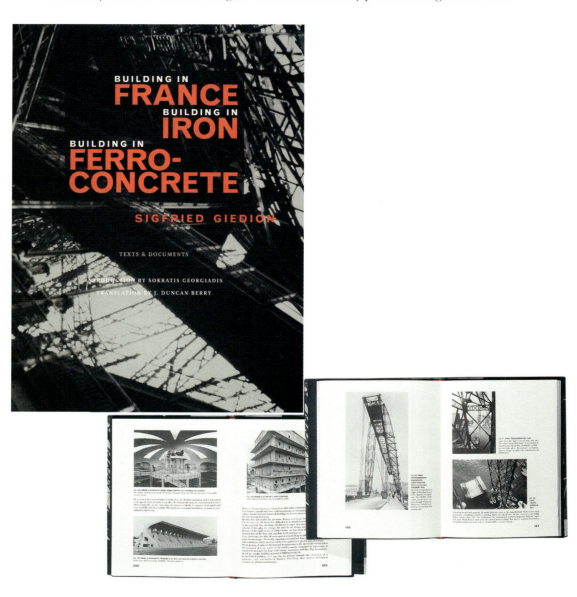

DESIGNERS Bruce Mau with Chris Rowat **DESIGN FIRM** Bruce Mau Design Inc. **CREATIVE DIRECTOR** Bruce Mau **CLIENT/PUBLISHER** The Getty Center for the History of Art and the Humanities **AUTHOR** Sigfried Giedion **PRINTER** Bowne of Toronto **PAPER MANUFACTURER** Weyerhaeuser **PAPER** Cougar Opaque, White and Natural **TYPOGRAPHER** Archetype

CHICAGO BOARD OF TRADE 1995

ANNUAL REPORT

ENTRANT'S COMMENTS The Chicago Board of Trade continues to be the global leader for transactions in market commodities, securities, financial instruments, and other products. This year's story focuses on the dynamic activity "in and out of the pit." A sequence of carefully selected "in" and "out" words supports this theme and builds a rhythm throughout the book. The pace of the book is also structured around simple black-and-white vignette drawings that support this year's highlights. Illustrative and gestural paintings serve as chapter openers and full-spread depictions. A unique accordian-fold pull-out details one of the biggest stories of the year – the expansion of the new trading floor.

DESIGNERS Curtis Schreiber, Fletcher Martin   DESIGN FIRM VSA Partners, Inc.   CREATIVE DIRECTOR Dana Arnett

CLIENT/PUBLISHER Chicago Board of Trade   WRITER Mark Prout   PHOTOGRAPHER Eric Hausman   ILLUSTRATOR Robert Clyde Anderson

PAINTER Philip Burke   PRINTER H. MacDonald Printing   PAPER Simpson Starwhite Archiva   TYPOGRAPHER VSA Partners, Inc.

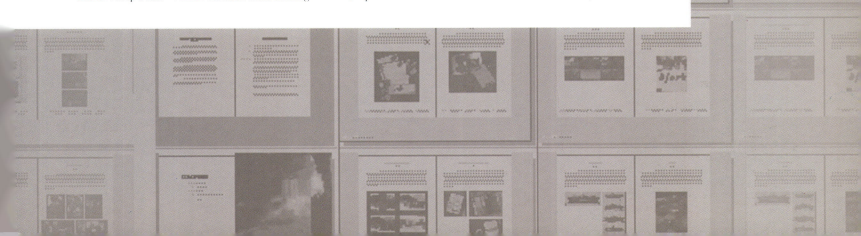

COMMUNITY AIDS COUNCIL

POSTERS

ENTRANT'S COMMENTS It's late. You've had a few beers. You've been cruising a guy and it's about to pay off. You walk out with your date, you see a poster – a hot guy doing what you're about to do. You see the condom. You remember to play it safe. There's no trick to these posters. They are posted in places where men meet men. Their purpose is to stop these men, get their attention, and show them how to love another man and not die from the experience. It's not about provacative images. It's about using what works to save lives and build self-esteem.

DESIGN FIRM After Hours Creative   CLIENT/PUBLISHER Community AIDS Council   PRINTER Heritage Graphics

WRITER After Hours Creative   PAPER MANUFACTURER Ingrim Productolith Book Gloss

PHOTOGRAPHERS Sue Bennett, Bob Carey, Bruce Racine, Rick Gayle, Tim Lanterman   TYPOGRAPHER After Hours Creative

INSIGHTS LECTURE SERIES

POSTER

ENTRANT'S COMMENTS This is a poster for a design lecture series sponsored by the AIGA Minnesota and the Walker Art Center which took place each Tuesday in March. Because there was no overall theme for the speakers, the poster merely shows a recognizable lecture image, the speakers' names and dates, and a touch of humor. The rest of the information, including speaker bios and registration information, is all on the back.

DESIGNERS Sharon Werner, Sarah Nelson   DESIGN FIRM Werner Design Werks Inc.   CREATIVE DIRECTOR Sharon Werner
CLIENT/PUBLISHER American Institute of Graphic Arts/Minnesota, Walker Art Center   PRINTER Heartland Graphics
PHOTOGRAPHER Darrell Eager   TYPOGRAPHER In-house

THE LIMITED, INC. 1994

ANNUAL REPORT

ENTRANT'S COMMENTS This year's theme of "customer intimacy" was told through various employee stories, actually shot as home videos, then printed as video grabs in the book. These quirky and humorous anecdotes convey the importance that the chairman places on customer service and teamwork, even as The Limited has grown into a $7.3 billion company with 4,800 stores.

DESIGNERS Arturo Aranda, Robert Wong DESIGN FIRM Frankfurt Balkind Partners CREATIVE DIRECTORS Kent Hunter, Aubrey Balkind

CLIENT/PUBLISHER The Limited, Inc. WRITER Robert Minkoff PRINTER Heritage Press PAPER Westvaco, Mead

PHOTOGRAPHER Brad Feinkopf STOCK PHOTOS Associated Press/Wide World Photos TYPOGRAPHER Frankfurt Balkind Partners

LOCAL INITIATIVES SUPPORT CORPORATION 1994

ANNUAL REPORT

ENTRANT'S COMMENTS   From its perforated, interactive cover to people stories and photos inside, the annual report reflects the non-elitist, participatory nature of this organization. LISC funnels public and private money into thirty-five program areas across the U.S., helping to rebuild housing and bring businesses back into the inner city. We asked photographers across the county to capture the "hidden good news" within these communities.

DESIGNERS Brett Gerstenblatt, Robert Wong   DESIGN FIRM Frankfurt Balkind Partners   CREATIVE DIRECTORS Kent Hunter, Aubrey Balkind   CLIENT/PUBLISHER Local Initiatives Support Corporation   WRITER Local Initiatives Support Corporation   PRINTER Heritage Press   PAPER Domtar Natural Jute   PHOTOGRAPHERS Deena DelZotto, Daniel Borris, Doug DuBois, Ann Giordano, Seth Greenwald, Mary Ellen Mark, Joseph Rodriguez, Tom Schierlitz, Matthew Septimus, Drake Sorey, Ethel Wolvovitz   TYPOGRAPHER Frankfurt Balkind Partners

ENTRANT'S COMMENTS The typeface Mrs Eaves, designed by Zuzana Licko, was inspired by the design of Baskerville. Named after John Baskerville's wife, Sarah Eaves, this revival aims both to retain those elements of Baskerville that have made it one of the most legible faces today, as well as to incorporate personal preferences. This booklet, produced to announce and promote the typeface's release, was directly inspired by the designs of John Baskerville's books, such as Aesop's Fables and the Virgil. This limited edition booklet was printed on a Heidelberg KSBA cylinder press by Peter Koch at his printship in Berkeley.

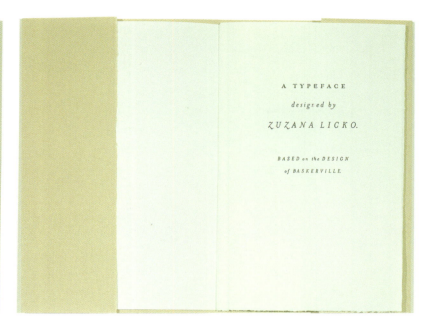

DESIGNERS Rudy VanderLans, Zuzana Licko **DESIGN FIRM** Emigre
CLIENT/PUBLISHER Emigre Fonts **WRITERS** Brian Schorn, Zuzana Licko **PRINTER** Peter Koch

NIKE JAPAN SOCCER HEROES

TELEVISION ADVERTISEMENT

ENTRANT'S COMMENTS Soccer has captured the imagination of the youth of Japan, and Nike has signed four of its brightest stars. This campaign consisted of television, print advertising, outdoor advertising, and point-of-purchase displays in Japan. The objective was to celebrate this affiliation with Japan's new generation of soccer stars and their impact on the future of the game.

DESIGN FIRM Wieden & Kennedy   CREATIVE DIRECTORS Dan Wieden, John C. Jay, Evelyn Monroe
CLIENT/PUBLISHER Nike Japan   WRITER Naoki Morita   ART DIRECTOR Young Kim

NIKE LA SEEDING

BILLBOARDS

ENTRANT'S COMMENTS The Nike LA campaign was created to recognize the unique heritage of winning basket-ball in that city. This specific effort was to seed that concept in the neighborhoods of Los Angeles through outdoor media.

DESIGNERS Imin Pao, Nicole Misiti DESIGN FIRM Wieden & Kennedy CREATIVE DIRECTOR Dan Wieden CLIENT/PUBLISHER Nike WRITER Jimmy Smith ART DIRECTOR John C. Jay PHOTOGRAPHER Brad Harris

SELECTED BY SOMI KIM ROBIN KINROSS J. ABBOTT MILLER

NIKE NYC COURTS

BILLBOARDS

ENTRANT'S COMMENTS Nike "NYC" is a multi-media effort to celebrate the special love of basketball in New York City. Nowhere does the sport reach such mythical status as it does in New York, where a single act of skill can live for decades beyond the actual moment. The "Courts" campaign paid homage to the famous neighborhood playground courts and the legends who played and made their reputations there.

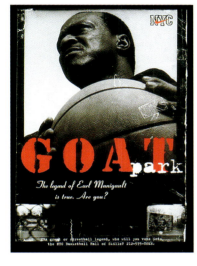
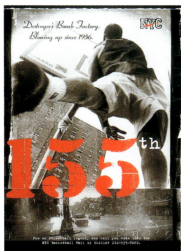

DESIGN FIRM Wieden & Kennedy CREATIVE DIRECTORS John C. Jay, Dan Wieden CLIENT/PUBLISHER Nike

WRITER Jimmy Smith ART DIRECTOR Young Kim PHOTOGRAPHER Exum

NIKE NYC LEGENDS

TELEVISION ADVERTISEMENT

ENTRANT'S COMMENTS Nike NYC is a multimedia effort to celebrate the special love of basketball in New York City. Nowhere does the sport reach such mythical status as it does in New York, where a single act of skill can live for decades beyond the actual moment. The "Legends" campaign pays homage to the famous neighborhood playground courts and the legendary figures who played and made their reputations there.

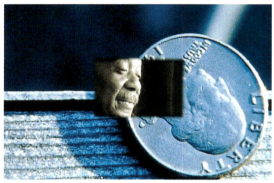

DESIGN FIRM Wieden & Kennedy   CREATIVE DIRECTORS Dan Wieden, John C. Jay   CLIENT/PUBLISHER Nike
WRITER Jimmy Smith   ART DIRECTOR Young Kim   DIRECTOR Robert Leacock   PRODUCTION MANAGER Jill Andresevic

PITTSBURGH AIDS TASK FORCE

ANNUAL REPORT

ENTRANT'S COMMENTS Designer's dilemma: celebrate an anniversary, or highlight the persistence of an epidemic? For an annual report that marked ten years of service by the Pittsburgh AIDS Task Force, we reached for balance. Portraits of people, who touched or were touched by PATF, humanize a double timeline that traces national events and local achievements.

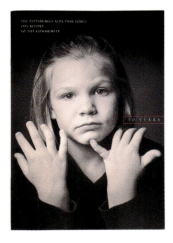  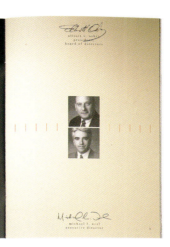

DESIGN AND PHOTO CONCEPT John Sotirakis   DESIGN FIRM Agnew Moyer Smith   CREATIVE DIRECTOR Reed Agnew

PHOTO DIRECTION Gina Rinhiuso   CLIENT/PUBLISHER Pittsburgh AIDS Task Force   WRITER Ann Z. Trondle

PRINTER Hoechstetter Printing Co.   PAPER S. D. Warren, Warren Dull   PORTAIT PHOTOGRAPHER Andrea London

TIMELINE PHOTOGRAPHER Michael Robinson   TYPOGRAPHER John Sotirakis

THE RED HOT BALL

POSTER

ENTRANT'S COMMENTS This invitation announced the seventh annual gala benefit for DIFFA/Chicago, which is the nation's largest fundraiser for HIV/AIDS service and educational programs. The excitement of the gala is revealed as the invitation unfolds as a poster depicting a flaming hot kiss on a gold metallic background. The black-tie affair is announced in black and gold letterforms representing the joining together of diverse groups of people in the common cause of fighting AIDS. They also provide a sense of flow and movement anticipated in an evening of cabaret.

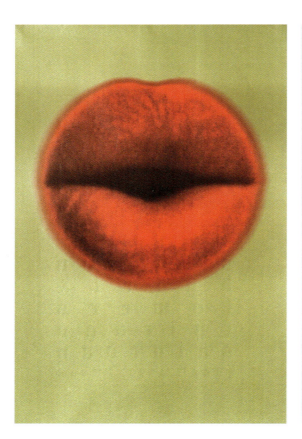 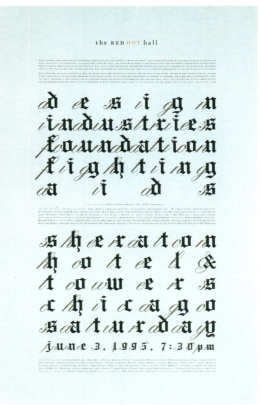

DESIGNER Ken Fox   DESIGN FIRM VSA Partners, Inc.   ART DIRECTOR Dana Arnett, Ken Fox

CLIENT/PUBLISHER Design Industries Foundation Fighting AIDS   PHOTO IMAGERY VSA Partners, Inc.

PRINTER Bradley Printing Co.   PAPER Domtar Natural Glass

SELECTED BY   SOMI KIM   ROBIN KINROSS   J. ABBOTT MILLER

RINGS

TELEVISION ADVERTISEMENT AND LAUNCH INSERT

ENTRANT'S COMMENTS (AD) To convey Coke's authentic Olympic heritage, we used archival photographs that locate Coca-Cola product and signage at past Olympic Games. Motion-control camera work builds a narrative sequence. Red circles animate on locating Coke product and signage within each image, anticipating both Coke's "button" logo (seen at the end of the spot) and the rings of the Olympics logo. A simple acoustic melody ("Rings") yields to a strong rock undercurrent at the end of the spot, a style that respects the unpretentious photography and gives the camera work momentum. A series of Olympic host cities and dates invests the tagline "Always" with specific meaning.

ENTRANT'S COMMENTS (LAUNCH INSERT) Archival photographs from past Olympics demonstrate Coca-Cola's historical presence at the Games. We chose images depicting Olympic fans since Coke's natural place is in the stands, not on the field. Within each photograph, red encircles Coke product or signage. Formally, the circles recall both the Olympics logo and the familiar Coke "button" logo. The word "Always" perforates the photographs, physically branding Coke onto the Olympics. We use the photos themselves—with simple captions—to ground the "Always" premise in historical truth. The sequence, cropping, bleed, use of white space, and red circle adapt these images to a contemporary purpose.

TOKYO 1964

MEXICO CITY 1968

FOR THE FANS

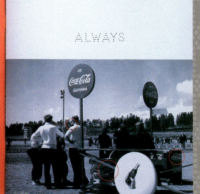

ALWAYS

DESIGNER Todd Waterbury   DESIGN FIRM Wieden & Kennedy   CREATIVE DIRECTORS Todd Waterbury, Peter Wegner

CLIENT/PUBLISHER The Coca-Cola Company   WRITER Peter Wegner   TELEVISION AD DIRECTORS Donna Pittman, Mark Hensley

PRINTER Graphic Arts Center (launch insert)   PAPER Silverado Suede (launch insert)   TYPOGRAPHER Pittman Hensely, Todd Waterbury

SEXUAL POLITICS

CATALOG

ENTRANT'S COMMENTS In this exhibition and catalog, Judy Chicago's controversial and monumental piece from 1979, "The Dinner Party", is contextualized in feminist art history. My intention was to convey the complexity, controversy, and emotion surrounding, not only this specific feminist work, but feminist work in general. Indeed, feminism itself. I chose to conceptualize the cover with a highly sexualized representation of an onion, which refers on various levels to some of Chicago's artistic concerns, but also typifies the bittersweet dialog engendered by feminist work. Inside the catalog, I wove an abstracted red vulva into the spine and text, constantly reminding viewers of the content that drives the exhibition.

DESIGN FIRM SoS, Los Angeles   DESIGNER Susan Silton   CLIENTS/PUBLISHERS UCLA at the Armand Hammer Museum and Cultural Center, University of California Press   SENIOR CURATOR Elizabeth Shepherd   GUEST CURATOR Amelia Jones   WRITERS Laura Cottingham, Amelia Jones, Susan Kandel, Anette Kubitza, Laura Meyer, Nancy Ring   PRINTER Overseas Printing Corp.

XIX AMENDMENT

INSTALLATION

ENTRANT'S COMMENTS The objective of this installation was to increase the seventy-fifth anniversary of the Nineteenth Amendment – while on a small budget and in an enormous room. The actual text of the one-sentence amendment was applied in eight-foot letters (9,936 point type) in vinyl floor graphics to the main waiting room of Grand Central Terminal in New York City. The general public could examine and walk on the law itself.

DESIGN FIRM Drenttel Doyle Partners   GRAPHIC DESIGNERS Stephen Doyle, Lisa Yee

CREATIVE DIRECTORS Stephen Doyle, William Drenttel, Miguel Oks   CLIENT New York State Division for Woman

ARCHITECTURAL DESIGNER James Hicks   PROJECT MANAGER Cameron Manning   FLOOR GRAPHICS 3M Floor Graphics

PHOTOGRAPHER Scott Frances

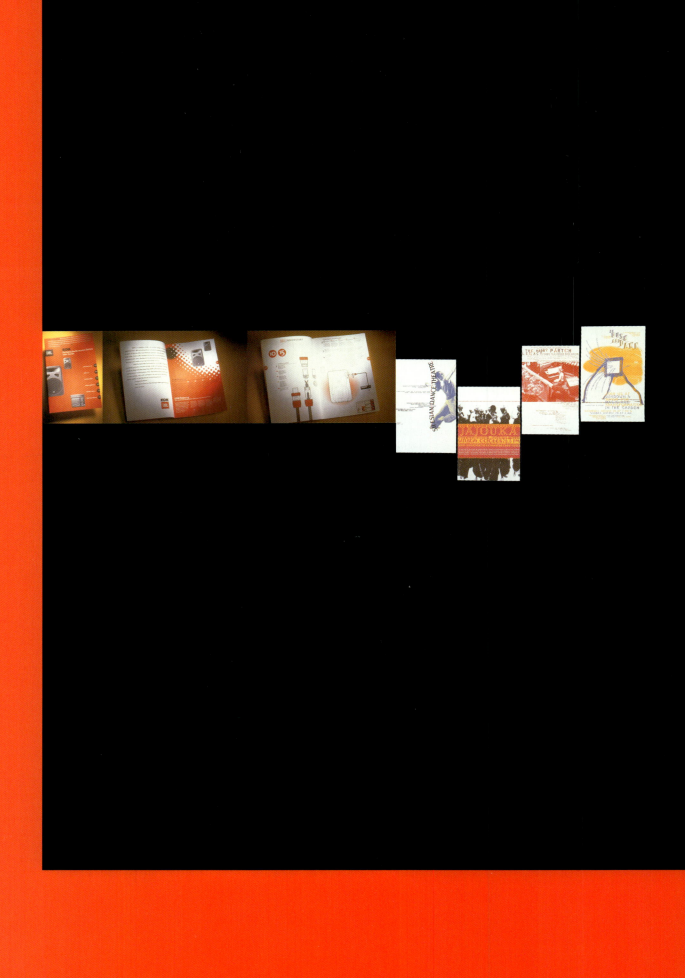

SOMI KIM

ROBIN KINROSS

JBL EON PORTABLE PERFORMANCE SERIES USER GUIDE

BROCHURE

ENTRANT'S COMMENTS Simplicity is the key for the JBL EON family of products. The user guide, or owner's manual, developed for the EON line is included with all products. In creating the user guide, more than 100 pages of information were consolidated into 28 pages. The layout, graphics, and typeface reflect a high-tech, yet user-friendly, feel. The cover also doubles as a table of contents for the main product sections. A detailed table of contents is listed inside the front cover. Products are grouped by operation. Each product section is designed to stand alone, and provides all the information needed to start using the product: a description of the product, a "quickstart" unit, and detailed technical specifications.

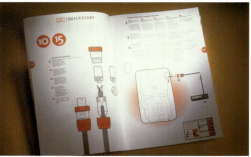

DESIGNERS Art Tran, Kate Murphy   DESIGN FIRM Fitch Inc.   ART DIRECTOR Jeff Pacione   CLIENT/PUBLISHER JBL Professional
WRITER Mark Henson   ILLUSTRATOR Francis Cozza   PRODUCTION Patrick Newbery
PHOTOGRAPHERS John Shotwell, Glen Cramer   DOCUMENTATION PHOTOGRAPHY Marc Steele – Fitch Inc.

WALKER ART CENTER

POSTER/MAILER SERIES

ENTRANT'S COMMENTS The Walker's audience is as broad and varied as its programming. Responsively, these posters must inform the "converted," as well as incite those audiences unfamiliar with the museum. They must function when folded down and mailed, as well as when posted in windows, on boards, and stapled to telephone poles throughout Minneapolis. Rather than approach the series as a set with a unifying identity applied throughout each poster, I kept the format a constant while letting the energy behind the individual performances (traditional modern dancy-dance; acid-trippy, exotic rock-n-roll; monotonal, dissonant racket; and G-rated, playful performance art) inform the typography, color, and image in the design.

DESIGNER Deborah Littlejohn DESIGN FIRM Walker Art Center CLIENT/PUBLISHER Performance Art Department, Walker Art Center DESIGN DIRECTOR Laurie Haycock Makela EDITOR Kathleen McLean PROJECT MANAGER Michelle Piranio PRINTER Offset-Insty Prints, Minneapolis PAPER Various

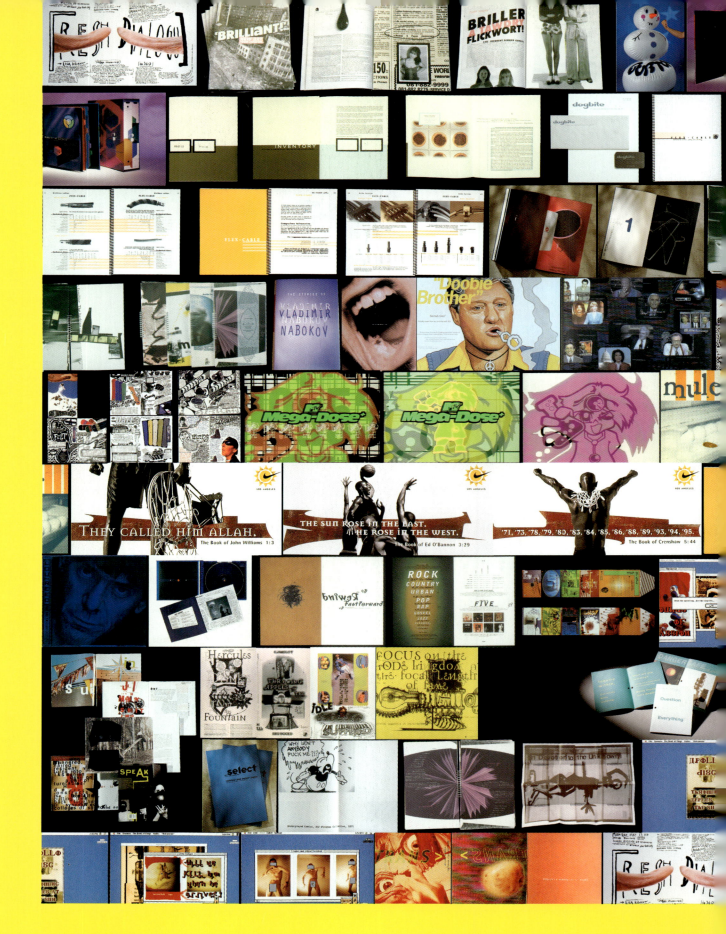

SOMI KIM*

SOMI KIM*

* I WONDER On the Saturday night between the two judging marathons, after opting for early bedtime

over a blues club, I fell into watching a PBS movie titled Signs and Wonders[1] from somewhere in the

middle to the end, thus staying up late despite myself. It was a melodrama about a dysfunctional family

consisting of a British vicar in a wheelchair who was transplanted to a working-class parish somewhere

in Central or South America, an estranged Marxist deconstructionist son who fell in with Neo-Fascists, an

estranged daughter who was brainwashed by a Christian cult, and the mother, who spent the balance of

the movie kidnapping back her daughter with the help of an American deprogrammer played with booming

intonation by James Earl Jones.[2]

The scene that hooked me was set in a diner in Malibu, where the kidnapped daughter tries to order breakfast with the encouragement of her mom, the deprogrammer, and invokes a childlike rhyme that warns of catastrophe should she ever leave the cult: "people will die, planes fall from the sky," said three young former cult members. The daughter is obviously disturbed and lapses into fugue states without warning, during which she sees apocalyptic landscapes of burning crosses. Choosing among standard diner breakfast fare proves to be too much for her thinly stretched psyche and overcome by hysteria, she is escorted from the premises.

Lying in a sterile hotel room that epitomizes corporate un-hip, with a psyche distended from the visual gluttony of the day, I felt complete empathy for many of the movie's characters and their assorted dilemmas: brainwashing, multiple belief systems, hallucinations, choices, choices, choices. The signs and wonders of the ACD 100 Show and other design shows point to a particular moment that is qualified by the participants, both entrants and judges. The moments, as recorded in annuals past, present, and future, show us something of a given year's memorable design works through the arcane filter of personal taste. It's much more exhilarating to be picked than to pick.

AMERICAN INSITUTE OF GRAPHIC ARTS
FRESH DIALOGUE

POSTER

ENTRANT'S COMMENTS Two tongues opposing each other are an obvious symbol for a design lecture called "Fresh Dialogue." Since we all have short tongues, photographer Tom Schierlitz bought two fresh cow tongues from the nearby meat market and shot them with the 4 x 5 camera. Somehow they came out phallic. We did not mind. Some AIGA members did.

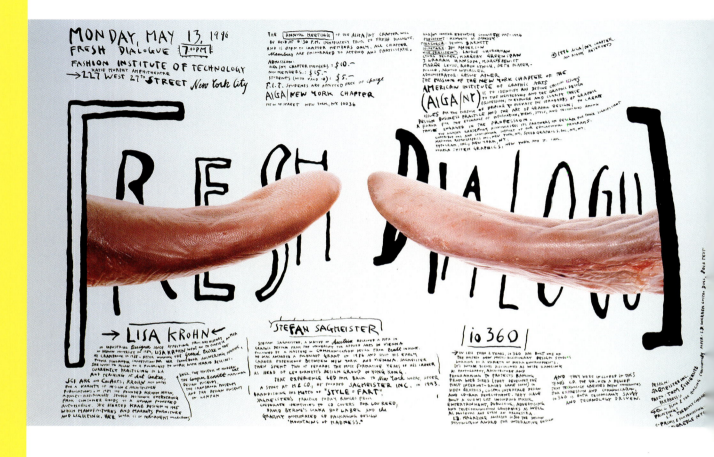

DESIGNER Stefan Sagmeister DESIGN FIRM Sagmeister Inc. CREATIVE DIRECTOR Stefan Sagmeister

CLIENT/PUBLISHER AIGA/New York Chapter WRITER Jim Anderson PRINTER L.P. Thebault Co.

PAPER S. D. Warren Lustro Dull Text PHOTOGRAPHER Tom Schierlitz TYPOGRAPHER Stefan Sagmeister

One of my favorite selections was the *Obscure Objects* magazine, which asks in its editorial note, "Is 'what' more important than 'how'? Is serendipity more important than plan? Is preconception more important than perception?... Is juxtaposition more important than what is inherent?" The pages of implied objects outlined with dotted lines suggest a crime scene, a coloring book, coupons, a Fluxus performance: a collection.

It was a heady experience to see so much design work laid out in endless rows during the ACD judging weekend. During the two days I ran through a broad array of emotions, from admiration to envy to disgust. Many of the more negative emotions were self-directed, as the hair-splitting, split-second decisions triggered an intensive bout of self-reflection. As the hours progressed, I threw out any attempt at consistency and informed subjectivity. I wish now that I had noted which items were picked on Day 1 and which on Day 2; my criteria for selection on the final day was much narrower. Shiny objects may initially wow the eye, but in excess tend to encourage a short attention span. Yet no more than a short attention span was possible, with 1600 entries to scan, at a rate of approximately half a minute per entry. General exposure to the ever-increasing speed of video/film

SELECTED BY SOMI KIM

BRILLANT! NEW ART FROM LONDON

EXHIBITION CATALOGUE

ENTRANT'S COMMENTS This catalog swiped the alien baby bird cage liner trash brash EXCLUSIVE! tabloid aesthetic and mindset to contextualize the current crop of young London artists growing up and coming of age under the thumb of the conservative Tory government.

DESIGNERS Matt Eller, Deborah Littlejohn, Santiago Piedrafita DESIGN FIRM Walker Art Center ART DIRECTOR Matt Ellerr

DESIGN DIRECTOR Laurie Haycock Makela PROJECT MANAGER Michelle Piranio CLIENT/PUBLISHER Walker Art Center

EDITORS Joan Rothfuss, Kathleen McClean, Douglas Fogel PRINT Web PAPER Newsprint PHOTOGRAPHER Glen Halvorson

edits helped us all digest meaning in micro-doses – otherwise we would probably have passed out after the first hour.

Reviewing the lists of selections, we judges made individually and in combinations, I'm not surprised that I managed to outdo everybody by sheer numbers. Sometimes assumptions about the inverse relationship between quality and quantity haunt me. My spree has more to do with collecting than indecision, though when racing through the rooms with volunteers pushing trash receptacles hot on our heels, I preferred to err on the side of excess. The timed process – induced flashbacks to feverishly filling blue books during college exams. I also recalled an assembly during Freshman Week at which the Dean of Students jokingly implied that one of us was a "mistake."

Most designers seem to be inveterate collectors of something, whether books, certain record labels, modern furniture, or dachshund replicas. In Lawrence Weschler's engrossing book, *Mr. Wilson's Cabinet of Wonder*[3], the description of a type of collection matched the process of the judging weekend: "Often there seemed to be no order whatsoever to the pell-mell pile, or none discernible to us, save that of continuous, compounding amaze-

PUNCHY THE SNOWMAN

POINT-OF-PURCHASE PROMOTION

ENTRANT'S COMMENTS Punchy the Snowman is ready for action. You punch him. He bounces back. Plus, he is a cool in-store point-of-purchase promotion for Burton Snowboards. Truly interactive.

DESIGNER David Covell DESIGN FIRM Jager DiPaolo Kemp Design CREATIVE DIRECTOR Michael Jager
CLIENT/PUBLISHER Burton Snowboards

ment." Wonder cabinets, Wunderkammern, private grab-bag precursors to museums, were commissioned in the 16th and early 17th centuries by European learned gentry boggled by the expanding horizons of their world. As quoted by Weschler, Francis Bacon described these collections as "... a goodly, huge cabinet, wherein whatsoever the hand of man by exquisite art or engine has made rare in stuff, form or motion; whatsoever singularity, chance and the shuffle of things hath produced; whatsoever Nature has wrought in things that want life and may be kept; shall be sorted and included." [4] Whether a wonder cabinet is organized by type of defect or with encyclopedic aspirations, it provides a telling glimpse into the ethos of a time and place and into the mind of the collector.

Design annuals are collections, judges themselves constitute a collection, and collecting is an active imposition of an ordering system on a group. As we know, this act creates seemingly natural groups that are anything but natural. Design competitions are flawed as collections from the outset, because the entries do not usually reflect the broadest range or the most challenging work. Then there is the difficulty of judging across media and design criteria: ad campaigns, broadcast graphics, stationery, books, and student

CANON

SALES TRAINING KIT

ENTRANT'S COMMENTS Canon's "Performance Development System" introductory kit was designed around Canon's corporate philosophy of kyosei, affirming the need for all people to live and work together for the common good. The "kit," layered in saturated colors, subtle satiny textures, and dream-like imagery of man, technology, and nature, is intended to generate involvement, reactions, registration, and excitement toward Canon's sales training programs. The new Canon sales training division's identity, which is structured from the geometry of the 120 building blocks found in nature, effectively focuses on the confluences of separate parts toward a common goal. At a time when technologies of copiers, fax machines, and graphics devices are revolutionizing the way we work, Canon's mission is to work closely with Canon dealer sales management, ownerships, and sales representatives to build product knowledge, selling skills, and technological insight, ensuring mutual success to all.

DESIGNERS Steve Farrar, Kirk James, Richard Curren, Karin Johnson, Chris Bradley, Cindy Steinberg, Shannon Poplin
DESIGN FIRM Jager DiPaola Kemp Design CREATIVE DIRECTOR Michael Jager ART DIRECTOR Steve Farrar CLIENT/PUBLISHER Canon
PRINTER O'Keefe, Deridder, Promotional Concepts PHOTOGRAPHER White – Packert Photography TYPOGRAPHER In-house

projects, all in the same pool. Some competitions operate with consensus as the final arbiter: if you alone cast a pebble for a piece, then you alone will mourn its exclusion. More interesting are shows such as the ACD 100, in which judges are able to select entries independently. Sometimes the result can be a competition within the competition, with judges racing each other to place dibs on their favorites, perhaps trading pieces like kids with Halloween candy. Other times, as in our case, joint selections are allowed, even encouraged, to reinforce the overlaps among judges' criteria. Sweeping through the IBM cafeteria, we hunted and gathered,

separating the edible from the inedible. One person's cake was another person's Wonder Bread.

When adding to my growing "collection," I found myself equally attracted to work that fell outside my realm of professional experience as to work that seemed like an old friend because I continue to cut my teeth on it. There were, in the end, perhaps too many annual reports among my choices – entries that, if they were human, wouldn't melt butter in their mouths. I can buy a skillful sell. There were perhaps two too many megacorporate ad campaigns... What bothered me most in retrospect was the realization that some selec-

INVENTORY: SELECTIONS AND
EVOLUTIONS BY JOHN SALVEST AND MICHALE BANICKI

CATALOG

ENTRANT'S COMMENTS The concepts of ritualized accumulation and numeration, found in both artists' works, formed the conceptual foundation for this design. Following the writers' lead of an essay written in five distinct parts, I chose to enumerate each line of the text. Details of artwork mentioned in each section precede the text – works before words. One thousand copies were hand-stamped and dated during the opening, allowing the catalogs to accumulate on tables in the gallery. The catalog situates itself in the exhibitionary space of the gallery as both document and participant.

DESIGNER Andrew Blauvelt   DESIGN FIRM Andrew Blauvelt   CLIENT/PUBLISHER Chastain Gallery
WRITERS Felicia Fester, Debra Wilbur   PRINTER Transamerica   PHOTOGRAPHER Various

tions will attain a certain cachet - flavor of the year? – due to the deep pockets for entry fees of certain, mostly larger, design studios, agencies, or clients.

I was partial to publications that brought multiple voices together, whether in the form of a magazine, catalog, or paper promotion. I was drawn to work with important topical content, such as the Community AIDS posters, Community Design Management resource guidebook, The Voice of the Homeless environmental communication, the 19th Amendment installation[5], and the Sexual Politics catalog. Humor is an important part of my work and something that

I am attracted to in its various forms, from silly visual puns and clever one-liners to dry whimsy. In the future I hope that CD-ROMs and Web sites will be viewed live, not on videotape, since it is difficult to judge interactive media indirectly.

I now know how very subjective the judging process is, subject matter can easily push as many buttons as the actual design of a piece. Singular images seemed rare and easily seduced me, as in the Red Hot Ball poster, the Lou Reed poster, the Fresh Dialogue poster, and the Nike LA Seeding billboards. I loved the intriguing pastiche of retropop glam and product shots in the Cornershop CD

CONVIVIALITY: FLIRTATION, DISPLEASURE AND THE HOSPITABLE IN THE VISUAL ARTS

ENTRANT'S COMMENTS The basic approach for designing this book was to create a situation where seven seemingly artistic and critical propositions could cohabitate under one cover. The main stylistic concern of the book was to make the disparate visual languages chosen by its contributors the strength and purpose of the title *Conviviality* and not a haphazard postmodern exercise in language. As a book about communication and experimentation in the visual arts, a pictorial introduction was invented. It was made up solely of historical examples of "models of cohabitation" in both art and architecture in order to set the stage for looking at its contents. Because of budgetary limitations, I used an overall aesthetic of simplicity—from the color palette to the level of reproduction—using black, white, blue, red, and an overall flatness as characters for portraying conviviality. The only departure from this theme was the silver stamped hard cover exterior, which resembles a cross between a shopping bag from Barney's New York and an illustrated industrial manual.

DESIGNER Mitchell Kane   DESIGN FIRM Marsupial   CREATIVE DIRECTOR Mitchell Kane   CLIENT/PUBLISHER Hirsch Foundation
CONTRIBUTORS William Braham, Joshua Decter, Lee Paterson, Laurent Joubert, Skall, Stephen Prina, Mitchell Kane, Françoise-Claire Prodhon
ILLUSTRATOR Mitchell Kane   PRINTER Production Press Inc.   PAPER Primopaque Matte Offset

package. Rounding out the ranks, the Muller 7-inch single, K2 Snowboard zine, and MTV Megadose graphics have an edginess and energy that invited picking like a really good scab.

I wonder whether any of us could articulate why some fine examples of design failed to make the final cuts. The immediate context of an entry could work for or against it, as style mongrels rubbed elbows with inbred puppy farm issue. Fleas and cooties moved freely among adjacent entries. Human cognition is susceptible to visual manipulation; as designers we are well aware that colors can be enhanced or squelched by proxim-

ity to others. Though my criteria shifted from hour to hour, many of my selections share typographic wit and strong vital signs, tactile appeal, and dexterity with integration of type and image. Lush, digital density, industrial chic, and a generic plainness are present in my consistently eclectic collection.

"Think of your work and think of what's going on around you." That's the epigraph to one of my favorite design annuals, titled Business As Usual, the 14th Annual Type Directors Club Show [6] from 1968. I bought it for $5 out of a bin of ephemera at a second-hand bookstore here in Los Angeles. It's an unassuming

DOGBITE

IDENTITY

ENTRANT'S COMMENTS Dogbite is a firm that designs and produces furniture and interiors. We wanted its identity to be sympathetic with prominent qualities in its work, such as tension and compression, folding, and its signature material– metal. Inspiration for the wordmark came from the client's references, as well as from our own investigations–Kubrick's "2001," Jacques Cousteau, space-age-bachelor-pad lettering from Stuttgart storefronts, and rave ephemera. The business card is thin, tempered stainless steel with etched type. The flexible material and radius corners make it wallet-safe and reminiscent of that classic designer's tool, the erasing shield.

DESIGNERS Kathleen Oginski, Greg Van Alstyne   CLIENT/PUBLISHER Dogbite

PRINTERS Wood Printing; Toronto Nameplate & Manufacturing Co.   MATERIAL BUSINESS CARD 0.006 surgical stainless steel

PAPER Hopper   TYPOGRAPHER Kathleen Oginski, Greg Van Alstyne   PHOTOGRAPHER John Howarth

white saddle-stitched brochure, 8.5 x 11, with a tiny photo on the front cover of a Newark riot cop pinning down or checking the pulse of an African American boy lying on the street. The intro (and only editorial text) states: "The theme of the 14th Annual Type Directors Show is 'Typography Wherever It Exists.' It's still the theme. We've just expanded the theme. Added a larger context. Look at the winners for their excellence in type direction. That's how they were judged. If the news-photos seem to overshadow the show's winners, think of how it is in real life." Printed in black throughout, small reproductions of the selections are interspersed

FLEX-CABLE

CATALOG

ENTRANT'S COMMENTS   The intent of the Flex-Cable catalog was to make an industrial catalog that looked like an industrial catalog, with historical respect for what has been done in the past as well as current industrial vernacular. Using contemporary type that bears a resemblance to bent cables, as well as using neon safety orange ink that jumps out under shop lights, I attempted to give the catalog a fresh look from a designer's standpoint while appealing to the sensibilities of engineers and forepersons who use the catalog.

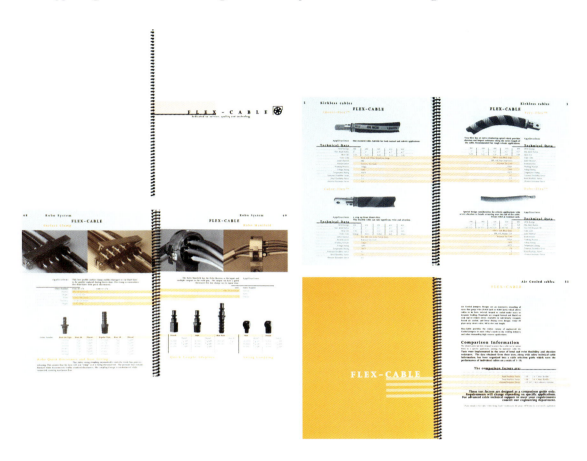

DESIGNER Craig Steen   DESIGN FIRM D is for Design   CLIENT/PUBLISHER Flex-Cable   WRITERS Various engineers and sales reps

ILLUSTRATORS Various engineers   PRINTER Oakland Printing   PAPER S.D. Warren Patina Matte

PHOTOGRAPHER 7th Generation Photographic   TYPOGRAPHER Eric Gill (Joanna); Rudy Vanderlans (Suburban)

with full-bleed photos showing antiwar demonstrations and race riots in America, starving children in Vietnam or Cambodia, dead soldiers, Dr. Martin Luther King, Jr., President Lyndon B. Johnson, Senator Robert Kennedy. Jarring juxtapositions result: a naked, emaciated baby on the page facing a perfume ad with a naked woman under the headline "The Body"; an entry to a paper company contest titled "A Call for Arms" next to a pile of dead soldiers on the tailgate of a transport truck; a melée involving students and police opposite a poster for a play titled "Riot," with the tagline "I'm gonna kill everything that moves and is black!" To me this TDC cat-

ENTRANT'S COMMENTS The indoor/outdoor environmental concept developed for the Circa Select booklet aims to establish the universal appeal and broad range of applications of the Select line of papers through a series of playful analogies. Communicators in business or commercial environments choose from the Circa Select palette to enhance any of their communication needs, ranging from internal communications to materials directed at mass-markets. The causal play on the "environmental" friendliness of these ecologically-sound papers follows as a subtle bonus to the primary notion that whatever the venue, the application of these papers is unlimited.

DESIGNERS Steve Tolleson, Jennifer Sterling DESIGN FIRM Tolleson Design CREATIVE DIRECTOR Steve Tolleson CLIENT/PUBLISHER Fox River Paper
WRITER Lindsay Beaman PRINTER Diversified Graphics PAPER Fox River Circa Select PHOTOGRAPHERS Various TYPOGRAPHER Tolleson Design

alog is a wonder cabinet of a particular moment in 1968 with its attendant typographic and historic horrors and wonders.

Is Business as Usual an exercise in cynicism or an idealistic wake-up call? Its sense of activism is endemic to the '60s and seems foreign to my jaded sensibilities. As an artifact, it's a spin on the kissing cousins relationship between ethnographic collections and visual collages, simultaneously deliberate and arbitrary. In the news media today, "business as usual" means that more exposure is given to criminal acts than to active efforts to address ongoing inequities. High profile trials generate a booming souvenir industry, including Jell-O portrait molds of a certain judge. My recent acquisition of a cable-ready television and "basic" cable subscription has widened my access to the signs and wonders broadcast to/through/at innumerable fellow consumers. Not even the mute button on the remote can save me from a hypnagogic stupor during which representations of idealized products and people brainwash me into choosing a new cereal, beverage, beauty aid. (Thankfully I won't have to write an essay about those choices.) The boob tube is a wonder cabinet, too, its collection a kind of superstore of longing. Sitting and surfing in front of another screen I note that despite its

GILBERT PAPER

PROMOTIONAL BOOK AND POSTER

ENTRANT'S COMMENTS The concept of the promotion, aside from the examination of a group of individuals working together, is the exploration of the idea of the "book." In terms of the physical nature of paper and books,
the piece stretches the format of a traditional book; the structure was designed without a set beginning or end.
In the 5,000 that were produced, every 312th book closes at a different spread; and each spread could be the
cover. The book also examines the direction of reading, and the way in which each page covers the next page,
either hiding or providing clues as to what comes next . . .

DESIGNERS, WRITERS, PHOTOGRAPHERS, ILLUSTRATORS, TYPOGRAPHERS Rob Bonds, Fred Bower, Elliott Peter Earls, Denise Heckman, Callie Johnson,
Sandra Kelch, Fiona McGettigan, Brenda Rotheiser, Brian Schorn, David Shields, Brian Smith, Corinna Stammen, Susanna Stieff, Martin Venesky
DESIGN FIRM Cranbrook Academy of Art, Design Department CREATIVE DIRECTOR Brenda Rotheiser CLIENT/PUBLISHER Gilbert Paper
DESIGN COORDINATION Katherine McCoy PRINTER TCR/Carqueville Graphics PAPER Gilbert Paper

democratizing promise, the World Wide Web hasn't yet encouraged me to increase my global thoughts or local acts. In the
professional context of design, socially conscious work is often
low-budget work or "cultural" work.

I suspect that designers who devote themselves to a particular
civic or social agenda might not easily cough up the fees required
to enter design competitions. The larger studios that can afford
"pro bono" work can also invest in efforts to make sure that such
work is noticed. Lines between good guys and bad guys are
blurred as cultural events receive funding from tobacco compa-

nies and certain corporations are vilified, despite questionable practices in our own backyards. If this 100 Show were to "expand the
theme" and add a larger context," what images would not provoke
cynicism or diatribes against self-serving do-gooders? Imagine one
scenario: Benetton's Colors magazine interleaved with the ACD 100
Show book, a giant clothing company ad recontextualized to split its
seamless seams and including a sampling of design hits, like those
old book or record club ads with their multitude of little covers, hook-
ing the collector in you.

ENTRANT'S COMMENTS The theme of this annual report is "The Voice of Jacor. It is large." The visual approach represents Jacor's off-the-air voice. It is a display of the images, impressions, and messages Jacor delivers through its publicity, promotions, and advertising. In the markets served by its 50-plus radio stations, this presence is bigger, and often grittier than life. Our objective was to create an annual report that captured the essence of this. In addition, this was a big year for Jacor. It announced mergers and acquisitions totaling one billion dollars, thrusting it from the number nine spot to the number four spot of radio companies in America. In effect, it became a very big player in the radio industry.

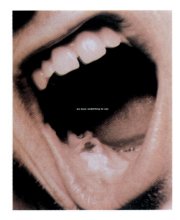

DESIGNERS Robert Petrick, Laura Ress   DESIGN FIRM Petrick Design   CREATIVE DIRECTOR Robert Petrick
CLIENT/PUBLISHER Jacor Communications, Inc.   WRITER Kirk Brewer   ILLUSTRATOR Mark Heckman (Clinton), various
PRINTER The Hennegan Company   PAPER Finch, Fine VHF   PHOTOGRAPHERS Paul Elledge (cover), various

[1] Back to that TV movie: All later attempts to gain information about this movie were fruitless. I got as far as the Masterpiece Theater branch of WGBH/Boston, by whom I was told that the program, titled "Signs and Wonders," isn't available on video. My request for credits and a synopsis wasn't answered, so I'm not really sure about pertinent production details or plot specifics. I began to realize that my interest in the movie was an elaborate digression (though not completely irrelevant) into the phenomonology of judging design competitions. Actually I'd almost always prefer to write about movies than about design! The aptness of the title led me back to an appreciation of the element of chance in collecting or in evaluating collections.

[2] Also the voice of Darth Vader. Was it really twenty years ago?

[3] Lawrence Weschler, Mr. Wilson's Cabinet of Wonder (New York: Pantheon Books, 1995) p. 82.

[4] Weschler, p. 76.

[5] I was struck by the end-papers. In the front: "1920 – The 19th Amendment gives women in the United States the right to vote." In the back: "1996 - Despite protests by students, faculty, and administrators, the University of California's Board of Regents votes to uphold its July 1995 decision to stop admitting students, hiring professors, and awarding contracts on the basis of race and sex."

[6] Business As Usual: Fourteenth Annual Type Directors Show, art directed by Jonah Nadler and written by Ira Redner, 1968.

K2 SNOWBOARD 1995–96

ZINE

ENTRANT'S COMMENTS The problem presented to us by our client, K2, was how to design with a ton of information and product within a tiny budget. Our solution was this low-budget, basement art "zine." We had a lot of fun working on it and snowboarders like it too. The riders consider themselves out of the mainstream and this piece had to reflect that attitude.

DESIGNERS Mike Strassburger, Robynne Raye, Vittorio Costarella, George Estrada   DESIGN FIRM Modern Dog

CREATIVE DIRECTORS Brent, Hayley & Luke   CLIENT/PUBLISHER K2 Snowboards   WRITER Modern Dog staff, Luke Edgar

ILLUSTRATOR Mike Strassburger, Robynne Raye, Vittorio Costarella, George Estrada   PRINTER Valco

PAPER Simpson Evergreen Matte   PHOTOGRAPHERS Eric Berger, Jeff Curtes, Aarron Sedway, Jimmy Clarke, Reuben Sanchez

TYPOGRAPHERS Mike Strassburger, Robynne Raye, Vittorio Costarella, George Estrada

MTV MEGADOSE

GRAPHICS

While much of the world embraces rave/techno-culture, the American media, by and large, have failed to recognize it. And although some American designers may be starting to mimic the look, they don't realize the aesthetic cannot be isolated from its context. Hence, the choice of the rave anthem: "You betta take this," became the inspiration for Dr. Sophia and a collaboration with The Designer's Republic. The look is a result of a certain sound. To separate the two would be to create a counterfeit. Because the show had the prospect of appearing worldwide, I wanted the packaging to escape the limits of traditional American TV design and to bring to the screen a sensitivity that had more international appeal and less about big fat 3D logos in your face.

DESIGNER William Heins   ILLUSTRATOR The Designer's Republic   PRODUCER Mara Marich
CLIENT/PUBLISHER MTV Networks

MULLER 7-INCH

RECORD COVER

ENTRANT'S COMMENTS In designing the Muller 7-inch single, we began by listening to the music. It was clear the music was American punk rock and we decided to create a cover based on the principles of punk that would also reflect the record label's "indie" quality. Our objectives were: to keep the cover simple (in punk you need three chords to play a song); to use a cut-and-paste style; and, most importantly, to keep it fun.

DESIGNER Michael Calleia   DESIGN FIRM Industrial Strength Design   CREATIVE DIRECTOR Michael Calleia
CLIENT/PUBLISHER Deep Elm Records   PRINTER Erika Records   PHOTOGRAPHERS Allyson Bice, Ande Lee
TYPOGRAPHER Industrial Strength Design

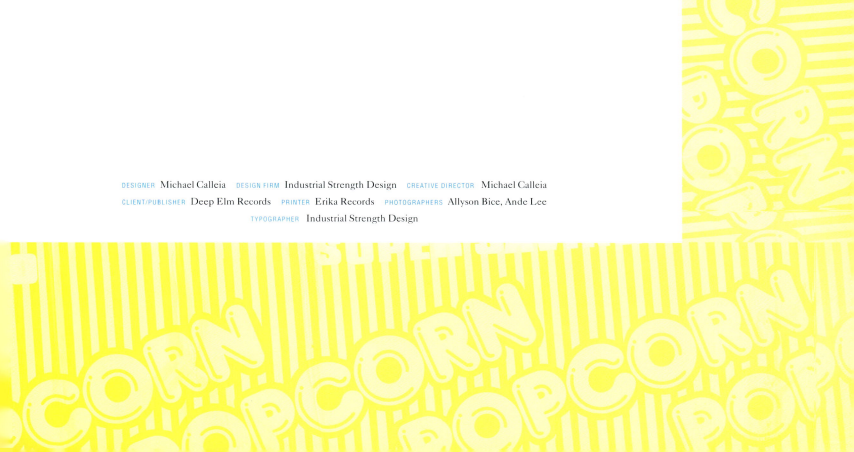

NIKE LA BOOKS II

BILLBOARDS

ENTRANT'S COMMENTS Basketball in Los Angeles has a rich history of winning traditions with its own legends and folklore. Nike's LA campaign was created specifically for the ballplayers of LA, to celebrate their style of play and winning legacy. Real legends, coaches, and their unique stories were used in each execution.

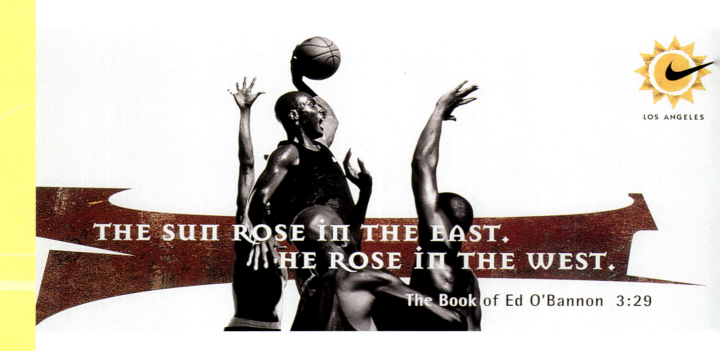

DESIGNER Jessie Huang   DESIGN FIRM Wieden & Kennedy   CREATIVE DIRECTORS Dan Wieden, John C. Jay   CLIENT/PUBLISHER Nike   WRITER Jimmy Smith   ART DIRECTOR Imin Pao   PHOTOGRAPHER John Huet

QUESTION EVERYTHING

BROCHURE

ENTRANT'S COMMENTS This booklet is the first in a series of five that uses different printing techniques to demonstrate how Plainfield Plus holds up under extreme conditions. Through visual juxtapositions and copy, the booklet prods designers and printers to "question everything" about their current paper to discover if it offers the extensive features and benefits of Plainfield Plus.

DESIGNER Alex Tylevich   DESIGN FIRM Thorburn Design   CREATIVE DIRECTOR Bill Thorburn   CLIENT/PUBLISHER Domtar

WRITER Kristine Larsen   PAPER Domtar Plainfield   PHOTOGRAPHERS Various

LOU REED "SET THE TWILIGHT REELING"

CD PACKAGING

ENTRANT'S COMMENTS The title song of Lou Reed's new album "Set the Twilight Reeling" talks about a star newly emerging. We tried to illustrate the metamorphosis from his dark prince character to a new-found man by using a deep blue-tinted jewel case in combination with a very brightly printed portrait of Lou on the booklet cover. Opened up, the back of the booklet, the design of the CD, and the tray card together form a diagram of an eclipse, the ultimate twilight. The typographic style inside reflects the content of the lyrics.

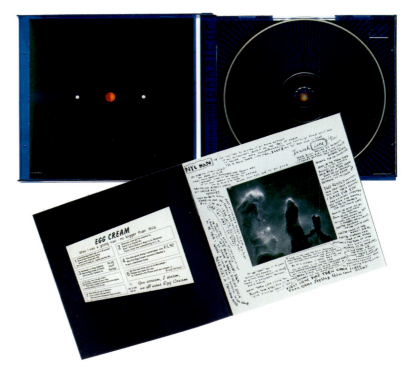

DESIGNERS Stefan Sagmeister, Veronica Oh   DESIGN FIRM Sagmeister Inc.   CREATIVE DIRECTOR Stefan Sagmeister
CLIENT/PUBLISHER Warner Bros. Records   WRITER Lou Reed   ILLUSTRATOR Tony Fitzpatrick   PRINTER WEA Manufacturing
PHOTOGRAPHER (COVER) Timothy Greenfield-Sanders   PHOTOGRAPHER'S EQUIPMENT Pete Corrish
PHOTOGRAPHERS (STAR BIRTH CLOUDS) NASA, J. Hester, P. Scowen   TYPOGRAPHERS Stefan Sagmeister, Veronica Oh

REWIND/FAST FORWARD 1995

ANNUAL REPORT

ENTRANT'S COMMENTS It took me three years to convince the executives of the Recording Industry Association of America that Amy Guip's photography wouldn't be too macabre for our annual report. When the photography was finished, I thought Amy's work struck just the right tone, particularly on some of our more emotional issues, such as censorship. To maintain the texture of Amy's work on pages where there were no images, color-test prints from Amy's studio were used as backgrounds. With powerful imagery, the design of the piece was about simple, black-and-white typography, and giving the photos space to breathe.

DESIGNER Neal Ashby   DESIGN FIRM Recording Industry Association of America   CREATIVE DIRECTOR Neal Ashby

CLIENT/PUBLISHER Recording Industry Association of America   WRITERS Fred Guthrie, Neal Ashby   PRINTER Steckel

PAPER Simpson Starwhite Vicksburg   PHOTOGRAPHER Amy Guip   TYPOGRAPHER Neal Ashby

Quousque tandem abutêre, Catilina, pati-

SEASONS GREETINGS

CHRISTMAS CARD

ENTRANT'S COMMENTS The parameters of this project were to make a festive greeting card that was not specific to a particular religion or holiday and that appealed to a large audience without being generic or cliché. It also had to showcase I.R.S. Record Co. so that viewers knew about its new building and its individual departments. In order to accommodate all of this in one card, I gathered inspiration from accordian-fold postcards that unfold to show the many aspects of one place. Each panel relates to the holiday and specific department, with the hope of engaging the viewer while still conveying the festive vibe of a greeting card.

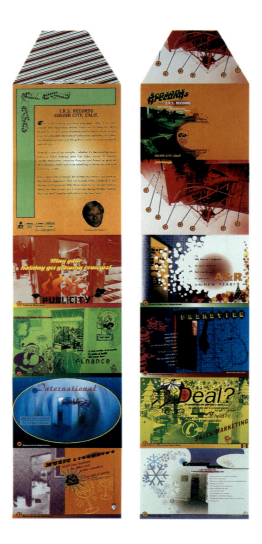

DESIGNER Emilie Burnham   CLIENT/PUBLISHER I.R.S. Record Co.   WRITERS Emilie Burnham, Mike Engstrom

PRINTER Anderson Printing   PAPER Hammermill Laurentine

SPEAK

MAGAZINE

ENTRANT'S COMMENTS The challenge of designing a magazine such as *Speak*, which attempts to reach the 18-29 age bracket, is to capture not only the attention, but the imagination and reverie of one's audience. Drifting upon the sea of articles that made up *Speak's* first issue, I floated a parade of personal images and curious typographies, as much hand-cut as computer-generated. These treats intersected and reflected the text, and the whole amalgamation is soaked with a personal energy, which I hope suggests a new, optimistic direction for today's youthful publications.

DESIGNER Martin Venezky   CLIENT/PUBLISHER Speak Magazine, Dan Rolleri   WRITERS Various   PRINTER BODY American Web   PRINTER COVER Lange Graphics   PAPER BODY Mira Matte   PAPER COVER Richgloss Book   PHOTOGRAPHERS Various

THE STORIES OF VLADIMIR NABOKOV

BOOK COVER

ENTRANT'S COMMENTS This cover makes reference to Nabokov the lepidopterist. This is a collection of his stories in one big package, just as he collected butterflies in a tray. The ghost-like specimen-mounted title is too pale to read. The reader is forced to read between the lines, an appropriate analogy for a master such as Nabokov.

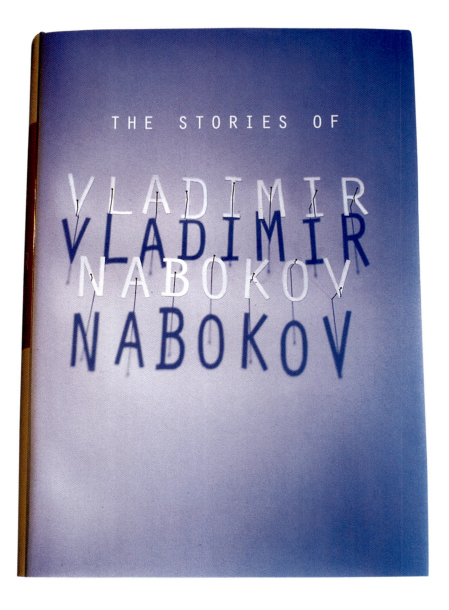

DESIGNER Stephen Doyle   DESIGN FIRM Drenttel Doyle Partners   CREATIVE DIRECTOR Stephen Doyle
CLIENT/PUBLISHER Knopf   WRITER Vladmir Nabokov

THROWING APPLES AT THE SUN

CD-ROM AND PACKAGING

ENTRANT'S COMMENTS I poke a pencil into the soft wood floor and snap the lead off. Why should you care? Because like spears flung at tomcats from passing cars, I speak volumes. Each one partially cross-referenced with the truth. Sometimes I'll put finger to paper like a pipe fitter, and make a mark deep and black like the red sun. How? I look through books, and in neighborhood trucks, carefully taking notes. I made this list for you:

1. Emote <u>while</u> you touch the paper.

2. Think hard.

3. Work like mamma never read you the story of patron saint John Henry

(the steel driving man who was born with, and who died with, a hammer in his hand).

And finally . . .

6. Make some money; it'll help with your other projects.

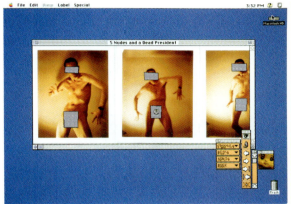 

DESIGNER Elliott Peter Earls   DESIGN FIRM The Apollo Program   WRITER Elliott Peter Earls

ILLUSTRATOR Elliott Peter Earls   PAPER Mohawk Vellum   PHOTOGRAPHER Elliott Peter Earls

MUSICIAN Elliott Peter Earls   PROGRAMMER Elliott Peter Earls   TYPOGRAPHER Elliott Peter Earls

TRANS>ARTS.CULTURES.MEDIA

MAGAZINE

ENTRANT'S COMMENTS: I based the design strategy of TRANS>arts.cultures.media on the relationship between the flow of information online and the development of the print magazine. The integrated design of the electronic and print magazine embodies the definition of TRANS – across, beyond, to another state or form – electronic information as it evolves from a fluid to a solid state. Liquid-like pages become the form of the publication as the text is presented in Spanish and English, allowing an interaction between voice and language. TRANS is the product of an electronic dialog. The challenge was to present the aesthetics and mechanics of ideas as they move through electronic means. Information-oriented, TRANS allows form to follow thought in an interactive and dynamic way.

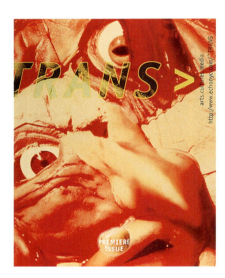 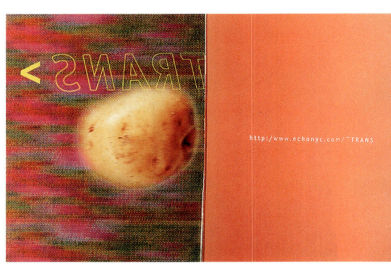

DESIGNERS Andrea Wollensak, Klaus Kempenaars   CREATIVE DIRECTOR Andrea Wollensak
CLIENT/PUBLISHER Passim Inc.   PRINTER Toppan

SOMI KIM

J. ABBOTT MILLER

DESIGNER David Lau   CLIENT/PUBLISHER Verve Records   ILLUSTRATOR Jonathan Rosen

eighteenth

COMMUNITY DESIGN MANAGEMENT

POSTER/MAILER SERIES

ENTRANT'S COMMENTS This book addresses a complex program of content through a constantly changing internal structure, while investigating historical and contemporary book design. The challenge here was to develop a design strategy capable of revealing a diverse range of content within a single cohesive volume that is more than 200 pages long. The resulting book employs a wide range of models including classical book design, flexible grid structures, and other distinctive types including "topic boxes," charts, and a lengthy bibliography. Within each of these broad categories, the design is further broken down revealing a number of unique details. This notion of multiple, localized design strategies is particularly relevant to the book's content in that a core aspect of the CDM program is providing distinctive design solutions for a wide range of community types. Consequently, the work is as much an investigation of book design as an effective vehicle for presenting content in a compelling and accessible manner.

DESIGNER John Rousseau **DESIGN FIRM** Rousseau **CLIENT/PUBLISHER** Design Michigan **WRITER** Jack Williamson **PRINTER** Signet Printing **PAPER** Consolidated Fortune

CORNERSHOP "WOMEN'S GOTTA HAVE IT"

CD PACKAGING

DESIGNER Deborah Norcross   CREATIVE DIRECTOR Deborah Norcross   CLIENT/PUBLISHER Warner Bros. Records

PHOTOGRAPHER INSIDE Deborah Norcross   PHOTOGRAPHER FRONT COVER Cati Gonzales

EXPD

ANNUAL REPORT

ENTRANT'S COMMENTS There are just too many annual reports that we call "people books." But when the opportunity came up to interview Expeditors International employees from nine different countries, we thought it would be interesting to do some unaffected shots while the interviews were underway: written and shot simultaneously, all in one day. White seamless in the morning, black seamless in the afternoon. Information compression continued with a four-page atlas that consolidated facts about new locations, financial performance, and the whole-current goodness of Internet and Intranet activities.

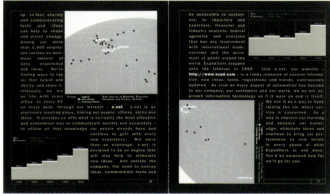

DESIGNERS Kerry Leimer, Marianne Li   DESIGN FIRM Leimer Cross Design Corp.   CREATIVE DIRECTOR Kerry Leimer   CLIENT/PUBLISHER Expeditors International of Washington Inc.   WRITER Kerry Leimer   PRINTER Lithographix Inc.   PHOTOGRAPHER Eric Myer   PAPER Potlatch Karma and Eloquence   TYPOGRAPHER Leimer Cross Design Corp.

LOU REED "SET THE TWILIGHT REELING"

POSTER

ENTRANT'S COMMENTS   I went to Soho and saw an exhibit of a Middle Eastern artist with lots of Arabic writing done directly on photographed hands and feet. It looked beautiful, sensible, and personal. We tried something similar (i.e. stole it) for the CD booklet lyrics for "Trade In," a very personal song on Lou's new album. Lou loved it. We made a poster out of it.

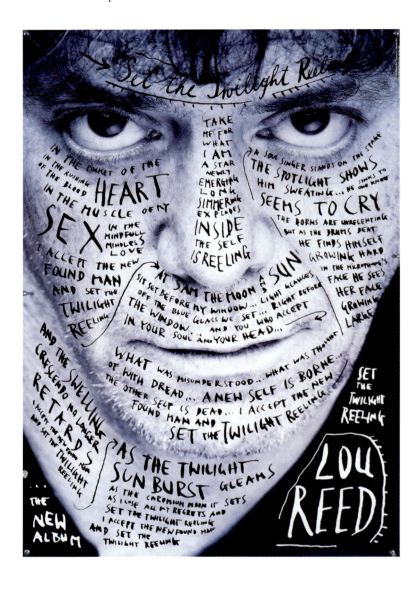

DESIGNER Stefan Sagmeister   **DESIGN FIRM** Sagmeister Inc.   **CREATIVE DIRECTOR** Stefan Sagmeister
CLIENT/PUBLISHER Warner Bros. Records   **WRITER** Lou Reed
PRINTER W.E.A. Manufacturing   **PAPER** S. D. Warren Matte
PHOTOGRAPHER Timothy Greenfield Sanders   **TYPOGRAPHER** Stefan Sagmeister

OBSCURE OBJECTS

MAGAZINE

ENTRANT'S COMMENTS The provocation is expressed through the cheap production, which is integral to the ephemeral nature of the content.

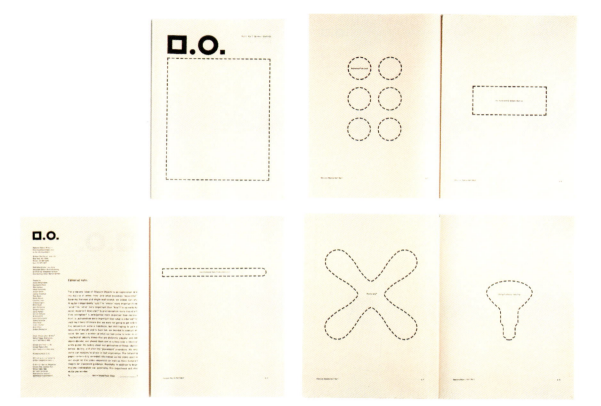

DESIGNER Alexander Gelman DESIGN FIRM Access Factory Inc. CREATIVE DIRECTOR Alexander Gelman CLIENT/PUBLISHER Obscure Objects WRITER Baruch Gorkin ILLUSTRATOR Alexander Gelman PRINTER Kim's Printing PAPER Newsprint TYPOGRAPHER Alexander Gelman

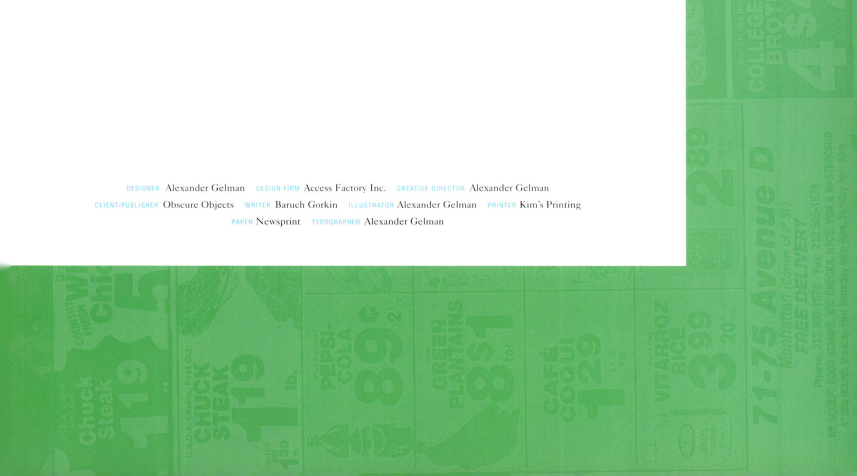

ROHOL

PACKAGING

ENTRANT'S COMMENTS Proclaimed an "industrial strength liqueur," Rohol's fossil fuel parody had to look serious to be funny.

DESIGNER Chad Hagen   DESIGN FIRM Thorburn Design   CREATIVE DIRECTOR Bill Thorburn

CLIENT/PUBLISHER Millenium   WRITER Matt Elhardt

SANDOVAL COUNTY SHERIFF'S POSSE RODEO

POSTER

ENTRANT'S COMMENTS The Sheriff's Posse Rodeo is an annual event hosted by the Sandoval County Sheriff's Department, New Mexico. It is a weekend of non-stop fun. The approach in doing the poster was to use elements familiar to the audience yet organize them in an unexpected, fresh way. I wanted to create a poster that would speak to its audience and visually challenge them as well.

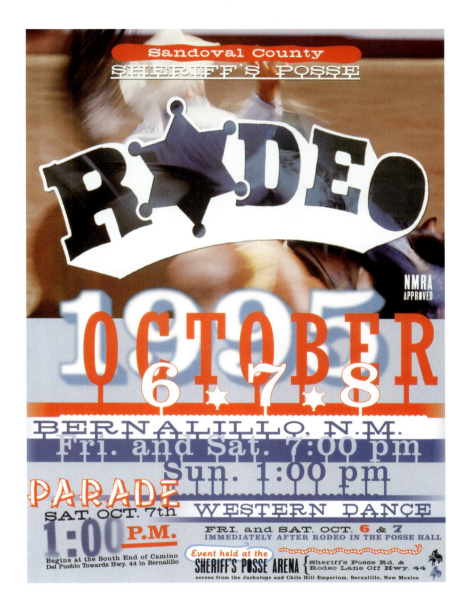

DESIGNER Greg Lindy   DESIGN FIRM REY International   CREATIVE DIRECTORS Michael Rey, Greg Lindy

CLIENT/PUBLISHER Sandoval County Sheriff's Posse   PRINTER Sorenson Graphics   PAPER New Oji Topkote Gloss Book   TYPOGRAPHER In-house

SEAGATE 1995

ANNUAL REPORT

ENTRANT'S COMMENTS Seagate is the world's leading independent manufacturer of hard disk drives. As computers start to resemble television with multimedia and audio-visual applications, the need for massive amounts of data storage multiplies. In the report design, we used computer vernacular graphics and pop global visuals to illustrate Seagate's powerful numbers and to make the complex world of data storage and management accessible.

DESIGNERS Yu Mei Tam, Robert Wong   DESIGN FIRM Frankfurt Balkind Partners   CREATIVE DIRECTORS Kent Hunter, Aubrey Balkind
CLIENT/PUBLISHER Seagate Technology, Inc.   WRITER Dana Longstreet   PRINTER Lithographix Inc.   PAPER Strathmore Elements Solids
PHOTOGRAPHERS Julie Powell, various   TYPOGRAPHER Frankfurt Balkind Partners

THE VOICE OF THE HOMELESS

ENVIRONMENTAL COMMUNICATIONS

ENTRANT'S COMMENTS The communal voice of the homeless community has been collected and composed in the Orientation Rotunda as an encircling frieze of inscriptions—nouns, adjectives, verbs—to form a spectrum of past, present, and future life choices. The Electronic Statement, an interactive electronic information system, empowers homeless individuals to exercise a public voice via vocational training in computer technology in response to the judgments of society (facing the downtown skyline of banks).

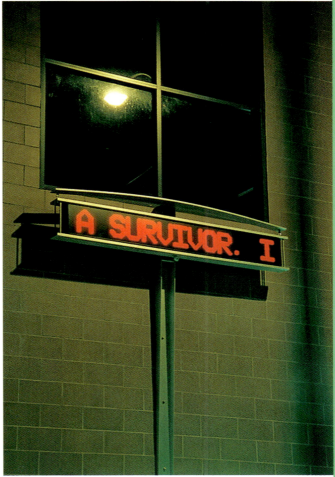

DESIGNER Joel Breaux   DESIGN FIRM BJ Krivanek Art + Design   DESIGN DIRECTOR BJ Krivanek

CLIENT/PUBLISHER The Union Rescue Mission—Los Angeles   WRITERS Residents of the Union Rescue Mission

TECHNICAL ASSISTANT Martha Najera   PHOTOGRAPHER Jeff Kurt Petersen   FUNDING The National Endowment for the Arts/

Design Arts Program, The Los Angeles Endowment for the Arts/Cultural Affairs Department

TRIDENT MICROSYSTEMS 1995

ANNUAL REPORT

ENTRANT'S COMMENTS Trident Microsystems designs, develops, and markets multimedia chipsets, graphical user interface (GUI) accelerators, and graphics controllers. To communicate that the company is enabling live video, and that they repositioned themselves in the marketplace, an animated message on the cover changes from "FOLLOW" to "LEAD." Inside the annual, Trident wanted to highlight the year's customer stories. The customers are included in the text, but we felt it was a more compelling story to feature the key strategies implemented by the company that led to its success. Video images are used to represent these strategies as well as the company's leading technology.

DESIGNER Bob Dinetz   DESIGN FIRM Cahan & Associates   CREATIVE DIRECTOR Bill Cahan   CLIENT/PUBLISHER Trident Microsystems Inc.
WRITER Tim Peters   PRINTER Grossberg Tyler   PAPER Vintage Velvet   PHOTOGRAPHER Various

VISUAL PROFESSIONAL

BROCHURE

ENTRANT'S COMMENTS This is a promotional brochure for Visual Professional, a company that produces hand-printed women's clothing, The clothing incorporates language, typography, and historical shapes into the surface designs and garment structure. The brochure is designed to suggest the printed subject matter and allude to the romantic nature of the clothes themselves. The structure of the brochure subtly reflects elements of the garment construction.

DESIGNERS James Sholly, Laura Lacy-Sholly   DESIGN FIRM Antenna   CLIENT/PUBLISHER Visual Professional   WRITER Candace Lorimer
PRINTER Design Printing   PAPER French Butcher Paper   PHOTOGRAPHERS Andrew Blauvelt, Candace Lorimer

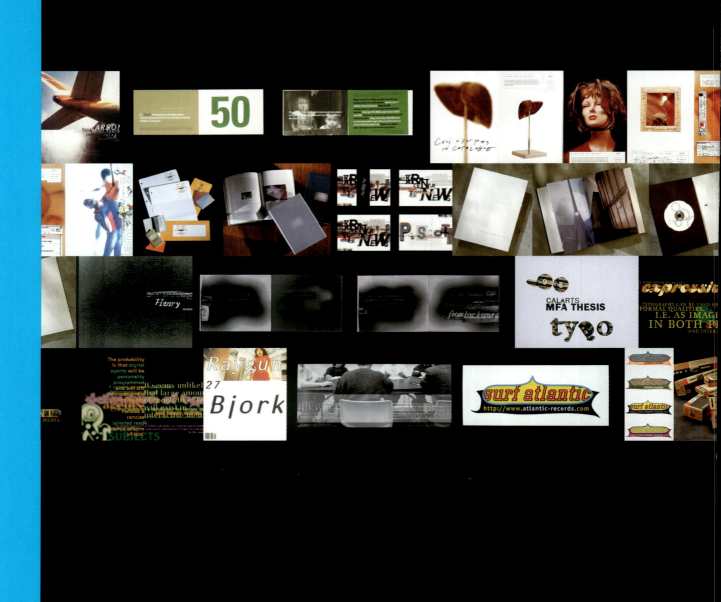

J. ABBOTT MILLER*

*GOOD ENOUGH DESIGN What about design in this rapidly waning decade? One is tempted to

draw large, millennial conclusions, to see in the cultural expressions of the passing moment some

key to the approaching shift in the calendar. But looking over these artifacts that have gathered

together for judgment, one thinks of them as children, offspring innocently hatched near the edge of

the world, unaware of the clock that ticks with tension and anxiety about the future. The psychologist

D. W. Winnicott crafted his theory of the "good enough mother" to describe a way of parenting that

seemed to yield healthy children and happy families. In contrast with overly attentive, hyper-nurturing

parents – often those of a first or only child – "good enough" parents give their kids some emotional

space in which to evolve, a space where mistakes are made, dangers encountered, and disappoint-

ments confronted and overcome. It is a space of discovery, independence, and negotiation.

The design I find myself drawn to in this painfully self-conscious, endlessly self-analyzing cultural moment is design that doesn't struggle too hard to become itself. These artifacts don't bear the burden of their makers' longing for immortality, for originality, for discovering the next thing, for birthing the next Beethoven.

Good enough design doesn't have competing layers of ambiguous meaning. It's not desperately clever or inexplicably angry. Mark Rakatanksy's poster for Iowa State University's Summer Institute in Architectural Theory, for instance, was made by an architect who is unintimidated by his lack of initiation into the curious rites of typographic culture; he has made a poster with a fresh, spatially dynamic design, and typography that is just good enough. Takaaki Matsumoto has catalogued the work of conceptual artist Felix Gonzalez-Torres in a manner that undermines the pomposity of the pampered, over-fed artbook genre. Sharon Werner and Sarah Nelson have created an identity package for a young copywriter that serenely and un-nostalgically inhabits the language of the dimestore stationery counter. Robert Petrick and Laura Ress have produced an annual report for Boise Cascade Office Products that builds informational tableaux out of the company's goods – pie charts are made

ART DIRECTORS CLUB OF TULSA

POSTER

ENTRANT'S COMMENTS This talk and poster kicked off what I jokingly referred to as the "end of print tour '96." After starting in Oklahoma, the "tour" went on to Sweden, Holland, Germany, New Zealand, Chile, Austria, Mexico, Ecuador, Switzerland, Nepal, London, Chicago, San Francisco, Detroit, Singapore, Milwaukee, and New York. For the poster, I used images taken on different trips. The top photo was taken in Barcelona while being bussed to another plane, and I forget where the bottom photo was taken. The words "end of print tour '96" disappear under the top photo and the type bleeds off the page in a way that indicates movement to me.

DESIGNER David Carson   DESIGN FIRM David Carson Design   CLIENT/PUBLISHER Art Directors Club of Tulsa

PRINTER Rodgers Litho   PHOTOGRAPHER David Carson   FONT DESIGNER Miles Newlyn

from looseleaf binders and bar charts from rows of filing cabinets. Because the idea is strong, the execution need only be good enough; in fact, on overly lavish, expressive approach to the type or photography would have diminished the clarity and directness of the final product.

Many of the best designs in this ACD 100 Show have been forced to deal with history. Called upon to document, preserve, and commemorate, these designs try to let history speak about itself. Rather than invent preciously updated "period styles," they invite artifacts and events into an open conversation with the present. Bruce

Mau's and Chris Rowat's design of Sigfried Gideon's book, *Building in France, Building in Iron, Building in Ferroconcrete*, is an elegant example of typographic parenting: the designers' challenge was to represent a 1928 text originally designed by its author. The text, now translated into English for the first time, has been visually translated into the contemporary culture of the book, in a manner that conserves the typographic structure of the historic artifact.

When Drenttel Doyle Partners were invited to create an exhibition in Grand Central Station celebrating the seventy-fifth anniversary of the 19th Amendment, the team decided to avoid the conventional

ENTRANT'S COMMENTS For the past fifty years, CARE has been synonymous with humanitarian aid, and the term "CARE package" has been absorbed into the daily vernacular. As with the most pro-bono clients, budgets are tight, resources are limited, and politics threaten to hinder the decision-making process. Yet, our three-year relationship with CARE has been one of mutual respect and common goals. Our firm has been proud not only to produce thoughtful work, but to promote an organization we truly believe in (Ted Fabella). The previous year celebrated CARE's fiftieth anniversary, this annual had to look toward the future. The theme, "Fifty Reasons to Believe in the Next Fifty Years" really drove the design. We wanted each statement throughout the book to command attention, and the faux newspaper wrap to convey a sense of immediacy (Rory Myers).

DESIGNERS Rory Myers, Kevin Kemmerly   DESIGN FIRM Wages Design   CREATIVE DIRECTORS Bob Wages, Ted Fabella

CLIENT/PUBLISHER CARE   WRITERS Matt De Galan, Erin Blair   PRINTER Bennett Graphics

educational exhibit approach, with its timelines, factoids, and photo panels, in favor of placing the text of the amendment, which asserted women's right to vote, across the vast floor of the station's main waiting room. The text itself – startlingly recent – is far more compelling than an aggregate list of women's struggles and achievements.

Susan Silton (SoS) has confronted the more immediate history of feminism in her catalogue for *Sexual Politics*, an exhibition which looks back at the artist Judy Chicago's 1979 project *The Dinner Party*. This monumental work featured a huge dinner table set with vagina/mandala ceramic plates and various embroidered tapestries. Chicago's approach was rejected by many younger feminists in the 1980s, who preferred a politically direct, language-based approach over Chicago's overtly biological and domestic depiction of women's culture. Susan Silton has been weaving feminist issues into her personal and professional work as a designer for several years now, and in this catalogue, she pays respect to Chicago's pioneering achievement while sowing some cooler, more contemporary vaginal imagery into the gutter of her book. Zuzana Licko's typeface *Mrs Eaves*, lovingly presented in a promo-

CECI N'EST PAS UN CATALOGUE

BROCHURE

ENTRANT'S COMMENTS In 1991, Bielenberg Design, under the pseudonym Virtual Telemetrix Inc., began a continuing series of self-initiated and self-funded creative projects that address issues related to the practice of graphic design. Previous pieces in the series include a book, annual report, poster, and T-shirt. Ceci n'est pas un catalogue is not a catalog. It satirizes the proliferation of designer-oriented product catalogs. Instead of actually buying a manufactured object, the recipient can enjoy the virtual experience of a conceptual product. "The more you know, the less you need." In keeping with the virtual theme, this piece was produced on a digital Indigo printing press, which doesn't require film, stripping, or plates.

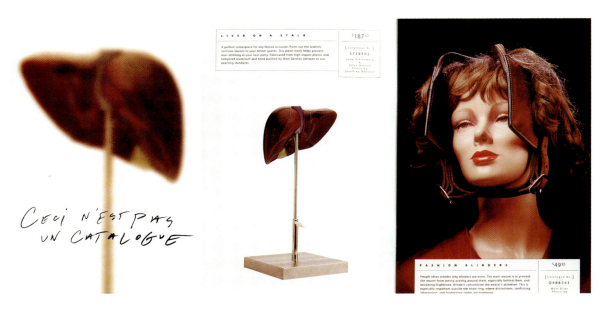

DESIGNERS John Bielenberg, Chuck Denison   DESIGN FIRM Bielenberg Design   CREATIVE DIRECTOR John Bielenberg

CLIENT/PUBLISHER Virtual Telemetrix   WRITER Chris Williams   ILLUSTRATORS Seymour Chwast, Ward Schumaker

CONTRIBUTORS Erik Adigard, Allen Ashton, Bob Aufuldish, Dave Betz, Brian Boram, Dennis Crowe, Paul Elledge, Matt Eller, Mark Fox, Pete Grannis, D. K. Holland, Jamie Koval, P. Scott Makela, Dave Mason, Pat Samata, Greg Samata, Jilly Simons, Rick Tharp, Geoffrey Wheeler

PRINTER D & K Printing (on a digital Indigo press)   PAPER S. D. Warren Lustro Dull   PHOTOGRAPHERS Various   TYPOGRAPHER Chuck Denison

tional booklet designed with Rudy VanderLans, brings a feminine lilt to the time-honored tradition of the typographic revival, a field in which designers aggressively comb the archives for the legitimate sources of mythic typefaces, attempting to one-up their peers and predecessors with truer versions of history. In place of such macho scholarship, Licko has created a deliberately interpretive revival, replete with fanciful ligatures and peculiar characters. She has named her font after Mrs. Eaves, the housekeeper and then wife of the esteemed eighteenth-century typographer John Baskerville. Most wives are also housekeepers, but few house-

keepers become wives; somewhere there is a lesson here about the husbandry of design and content, in which typographic form and layout create an environment – clean or cluttered – in which a text can blossom. Holding on to her own identity while fondly caring for the typographic past and present, *Mrs Eaves* is a good enough housekeeper.

The millennial clock is audibly ticking in one important piece of history included in the show: Agnew Moyer Smith's annual report for the *Pittsburgh AIDS Task Force*. The graphic marks of a time-line chronicling the impact of AIDS runs directly over the faces of

DANCE MONTH 1995

POSTER

ENTRANT'S COMMENTS The interplay of figures, type, and color on the front side of the poster represents an abstract choreography. The reverse side features a calendar of events for the month-long celebration.

DESIGNER Fritz Klaetke   DESIGN FIRM Visual Dialogue   CREATIVE DIRECTOR Fritz Klaetke
CLIENT/PUBLISHER The Dance Complex, Cambridge, Mass.   WRITER Rozann Kraus   PRINTER Pride Printers
PAPER Champion Carnival   PHOTOGRAPHER Charles Barclay Reeves   TYPOGRAPHER Fritz Klaetke

people whose lives have been shaped by the epidemic. Whereas timelines tend to represent the rhythm of years and decades as a neutral medium, this design makes time personal, palpable, and inescapably urgent.

Designers tend to associate the millennium with digital media, a magical field which promises either the cataclysmic end or the utopian rebirth of the profession. Several 100 Show winners took a low-tech approach to the supposedly hi-tech field of new media, confronting the Web as an arena of everyday life rather than a fetishized landscape of blinking lights and crossing wires.

Fritz Klaetke's stationery program for *Drawbridge*, a Web consulting and programming company, has a deliberately heavy, physical character that invokes the Web as a site of construction. For *Greenhood and Company*, another Web consultancy, Vrontikis Design Office has paired tactile paper stocks with laser printing and rubber stamps to create a "rapid prototype" for an identity that might quickly change its addresses and services in the uncertain years of its infancy. Looking back over the happy, healthy children who populate this year's ACD 100 Show, I am struck that while Somi Kim and Robin Kinross have shared only a few selections with each

RACHEL EAGER

STATIONARY SYSTEM

ENTRANT'S COMMENTS Rachel is a young copywriter just starting out and her identity system needed to be fresh, fun, functional, and affordable. The lined writing paper and composition books seem appropriate for her, having just graduated from school. Business cards as little composition books allow her to give out samples of her writing, which she can revise easily.

DESIGNERS Sharon Werner, Sarah Nelson   DESIGN FIRM Werner Design Werks Inc.

CREATIVE DIRECTOR Sharon Werner   CLIENT/PUBLISHER Rachel Eager, Copywriter   WRITER Rachel Eager

PRINTER Nomadic Press   PAPER Various   TYPOGRAPHER Sharon Werner

other, I am in solid agreement with each of them on a substantial number of pieces. Perhaps I have been a good enough juror. While Somi is part of the advance guard of West Coast design, and Robin is a sometimes solitary defender of typographic traditions, I entered design through the wayward liberalism of New York's design community, with its taste for language, history, and humor. I admire experimentation and respect tradition, but something wonderful happens when design is allowed to mix with the culture of ordinary life, free to make mistakes and find its own purpose.

FELIX GONZALEZ-TORRES

CATALOG

ENTRANT'S COMMENTS The catalog accompanied a one-month exhibition of the artist's work. The work is very personal and is meant to create a direct connection between the artist and the viewer. The designer felt, therefore, that a large, traditional coffee-table-style catalog would not be appropriate for Gonzalez-Torres' highly personal work. The book was designed more like a storybook than a picture book, which is reflected by the type treatment, structure, and size of the book.

DESIGNER Takaaki Matsumoto   DESIGN FIRM Matsumoto Incorporated   CREATIVE DIRECTOR Takaaki Matsumoto
CLIENT/PUBLISHER Solomon R. Guggenheim Museum   AUTHOR Nancy Spector   PRINTER Cantz (Germany)
PAPER BVS   PHOTOGRAPHER Various   TYPOGRAPHER Takaaki Matsumoto

FOR BETTER OR FOR WORSE: LECTURE BY THE MAKELAS

LECTURE

ENTRANT'S COMMENTS CS: The AIGA needed an announcement for a lecture by
P. Scott and Laurie Haycock Makela – two very individual designers who
happen to be husband and wife. So we decided to do a set of postcards.
FK: Visual Dialogue went to work on one for him . . .
CS: Stoltze Design designed her card.
FK: And for the third, we overprinted the two designs and silk-screened
"The Makelas" on top by hand.
CS: All wrapped up with a band proclaiming "For Better or For Worse."

DESIGNERS Fritz Klaetke, Eric Norman, Clifford Stoltze   DESIGN FIRMS Stoltze Design, Visual Dialogue
CLIENT/PUBLISHER American Institute of Graphic Arts/Boston   PRINTER Eastern Rainbow Inc.
PAPER Unisource   TYPOGRAPHER In-house

GATX CAPITAL CORPORATION 1995

ANNUAL REPORT AND CD

ENTRANT'S COMMENTS Drawing from a broad pool of specialties, GATX Capital compiles project-specific teams to satisfy the specialized needs of its customers. The seamless combination of a variety of talents and resources are depicted throughout the annual and CD as a series of contingent shapes, combining to represent a complete service, or as translucent layers that merge to reveal a unified (visual) solution.

DESIGNERS Steve Tolleson, Jean Orlebeke   DESIGN FIRM Tolleson Design   CREATIVE DIRECTOR Steve Tolleson

CLIENT/PUBLISHER GATX Capital Corporation   WRITER Rick Prince   CD PRGRAMMING Entasis

CD DESIGN AND ART DIRECTION Tolleson Design   PRINTER MacDonald Printing   PAPER Simpson Archiva, Gilbert Gilclear

PHOTOGRAPHERS Nickoli Zurek, Jeff Corwin   TYPOGRAPHER Tolleson Design

HENRY

BOOK

ENTRANT'S COMMENTS Inside and outside. Open and closed. Personal and universal. Intimate and undetermined. Each is defined by the other. In the form of my narrative, the reader becomes a collaborator as she is drawn into the dark forest. Texture and pattern reveal clues to the environment, creating an experience and a dialog of interpretation without confining it. The text takes on the emotion, volume, and speed of the spoken voice while a second text appears on the backside of the pages, embossed from the inside, exposing an inner voice that relates the undercurrent of the story.

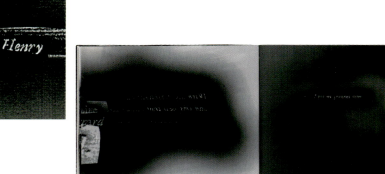

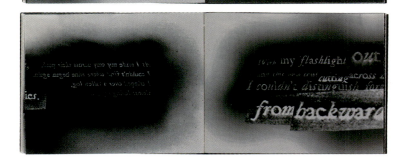

DESIGNER Kari Strand   DESIGN FIRM Cranbrook Academy of Art   WRITER Kari Strand

ILLUSTRATOR Kari Strand   PAPER Various   PHOTOGRAPHER Kari Strand   TYPOGRAPHER Kari Strand

HYPERTYPE

DIGITAL THESIS PROJECT

ENTRANT'S COMMENTS The project set out to discuss the possibilities for typography in an interactive, time-based medium. The design and writing are deliberately intertwined: the interface begins as 12-point text; then as each topic is discussed, it is illustrated on screen and becomes part of the interface. It grows in a linear, structured fashion toward the final section where users can wander freely in a typographic environment, choosing which subtopics they delve into further. The typography is deliberately eclectic and tries to encompass audio, motion, and time while retaining aspects of printed typography – composition, scale, detail, and word play.

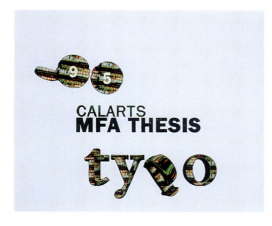

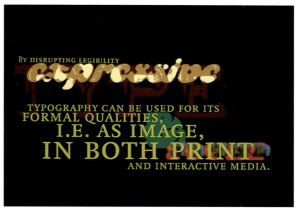

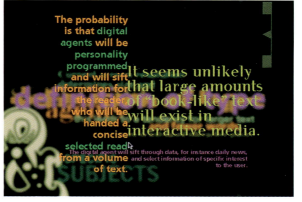

DESIGNER Michael Worthington   **CLIENT/PUBLISHER** Self-published   **WRITER** Michael Worthington   **TYPOGRAPHER** Michael Worthington

1995 SUMMER INSTITUTE IN ARCHITECTURAL THEORY

POSTER

ENTRANT'S COMMENTS YOU are (in) here. This poster uses a typical institutional scene – the seminar classroom – to explore questions of identity: the identity of YOU or ANOTHER projected into a future scene by means of a scene from the past; the identity (and repetition) of the classroom scene; the identity (and repetition) of an annual institute; the multiple identities of the participants; the multiple identities of the faculty, and so on. The type also seems to respond to the pressure of this "YOU", compressing as it approached either side of "YOU's" chair.

DESIGNER Mark Rakatansky   DESIGN ASSISTANT Brian Ziska   DESIGN FIRM Mark Rakatansky Studio

CLIENT/PUBLISHER Robert Segrest, Chair, Department of Architecture, Iowa State University   PRINTER Sigler Graphics

PAPER Northwet Gloss   PHOTOGRAPHER Greg Scheideman

BJORK

COVER

ENTRANT'S COMMENTS This cover was third in a series that simplified the approach to subject matter, but hopefully retained some freshness and relevance. The previous cover had the photo in a similar place but without any copy in the white space. Bjork is hitting her head on the ceiling in the photo and it seemed to make sense to have her at the top of the page. This is one of my favorite *Raygun* covers. It feels good.

music + style: end of print
june/july $3.95 can $4.50

DESIGNER David Carson   DESIGN FIRM David Carson Design   CLIENT/PUBLISHER Raygun Publishing

PHOTOGRAPHER Dave Stewart   FONT DESIGNER Miles Newlyn

SURF ATLANTIC

LOGO, IDENTITY, AND STICKERS

ENTRANT'S COMMENTS Have you ever seen those strange beautifully shaped black puffy pods from the ocean lying along the beach? They are the shells that house manta ray eggs. Beyond that, the rest is pretty direct:

surfing

Atlantic; the ocean

surf boards

"surf the net"

sea creatures

DESIGNER Brenda Rotheiser   DESIGN FIRM Atlantic Records Art Department   CREATIVE DIRECTOR Brenda Rotheiser

CLIENT/PUBLISHER Atlantic Records Multimedia Department   PRINTER Westbury Press   TYPOGRAPHER Brenda Rotheiser

YAKIMA

PACKAGING

ENTRANT'S COMMENTS Yakima produces a high quality, dependable roof racking system. The first objective of the new package design was to upgrade the look of the packaging to match the value of the products, but still be very simple and utilitarian to convey the Yakima design aesthetic. The second objective was to assist the consumer with the product features and component fitting using the icon system for easier references. The third objective was to reinforce Yakima's commitment to environmental responsibility by using a high percentage of post-consumer waste for packaging materials and inks.

DESIGNERS Kobe, Jeff Johnson, Alan Leusink   DESIGN FIRM Duffy Design

CREATIVE DIRECTOR Joe Duffy   CLIENT/PUBLISHER Yakima   ILLUSTRATOR Kobe

J. ABBOTT MILLER

ROBIN KINROSS

ALONE TOGETHER

CD PACKAGING

DESIGNER David Lau   DESIGN FIRM Verve Records   CREATIVE DIRECTOR   CLIENT/PUBLISHER Verve Records

PRINTER Shorewood   PHOTOGRAPHER Herman Leonard   TYPOGRAPHER David Lau

SELECTED BY   ROBIN KINROSS   J. ABBOTT MILLER

ANTONIO CARLOS JOBIM: THE MAN FROM IPANEMA

CD PACKAGING

ENTRANT'S COMMENTS Antonio Carlos Jobim turned to the beautiful surrounding of his native Brazil for inspiration to write his music. I also used them as inspiration to design the package for this three CD, 60 page booklet set. The double spiraled frosted PVC covered booklet uses only recycled colored paper to represent the tropical hues of the Brazilian coast, nature's elements, and Jobim's playfulness. The package also incorporates three non-glued CD sleeves die-cut to represent leaves, shells and fish to hold the CDs themthelves. Jobim's wife, Ana Lontra-Jobim, contributed much of the photography featured in this package.

DESIGNER Giulio Turturro   DESIGN FIRM Verve Records   CREATIVE DIRECTOR Giulio Turturro
CLIENT/PUBLISHER Verve Records   WRITERS Various   PRINTER Enterprise Press   PAPER Mohawk Satin
PHOTOGRAPHER Ana Lontra-Jobim   TYPOGRAPHER Giulio Turturro

CAL ARTS

INTERACTIVE CD-ROM

ENTRANT'S COMMENTS The CalArts Anniversary CDROM was designed with the intention of being an archive for work from all the disciplines at CalArts: Design, Photography, Theatre, Dance, Film, Art, Music and Critical Studies. It had to be simple and easy to use, since the primary audience (alumni) were unfamiliar with CDROMs, which meant a relatively straightforward interface. I tried to create a piece that though frequently historical, also showed CalArts as it is now: hence interviews with students and faculty both positive and negative. I was given free reign to create "my view" of CalArts, and having control over the content and the form enabled me to capture the energy, ambience and bizarre nature of this isolated breeding ground for art. I feel I was able to design a visual experience that was well researched, and informational, without becoming purely archival and dry in its presentation.

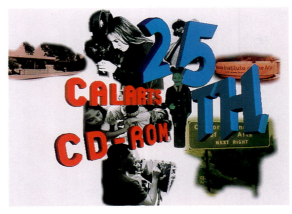

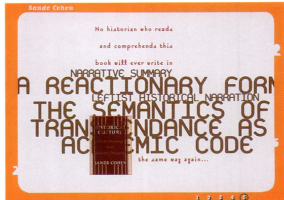

DESIGNERS Michael Worthington, Deborah Littlejohn   DESIGN FIRM Verve Records   CREATIVE DIRECTOR Michael Worthington   CLIENT/PUBLISHER California Institute of the Arts   WRITERS Various   ILLUSTRATORS Various   VIDEO FOOTAGE Farzao Karimi   PHOTOGRAPHERS Various   TYPOGRAPHERS Michael Worthington, Deborah Littlejohn

DOUBLETAKE ISSUES 1-4

MAGAZINES

ENTRANT'S COMMENTS In launching DoubleTake magazine, the editors hope to build and reach a community of those "devoted to the written word and the visual image, to renderings of the world as it is and as it might be." Publishing photography—and to some extent, writing—is a process of translation of the original work to the printed page. The goal driving the design was to arrive at the clearest representation of the work assembled, where devices of format and typography support, yet recede from the reading, allowing the word to come forward. The skill of the printer completes this collaborative effort.

DESIGNER Molly Renda   WRITERS Various   EDITORS Robert Coles, Alex Harris   PRINTER HarperPrints

PAPER Repap Lithofect Plus Recycled Dull   PHOTOGRAPHERS Various   TYPOGRAPHER DoubleTake Magazine

DRAWBRIDGE

IDENTITY

ENTRANT'S COMMENTS In the logo for this Web programming and consulting company, the word "drawbridge" metaphorically "spans the moat" of the confusing jumble of Web acronyms, providing the connection between the client and the Internet.

DESIGNER Fritz Klaetke   DESIGN FIRM Visual Dialogue   CREATIVE DIRECTOR Fritz Klaetke

CLIENT/PUBLISHER Drawbridge   WRITER Adam Buhler   PRINTERS Alpha Press, Shear Color Printing

PAPER Strathmore Elements, Clay-coated Newsback, Brown Kraft Packaging, Pacific Packaging

TYPOGRAPHER Fritz Klaetke

PAUL DRESHER ENSEMBLE

POSTER

ENTRANT'S COMMENTS This poster announces two music performances by the Paul Dresher Ensemble. The challenge was to communicate and to give equal importance to both events as well as reflect the experimental nature of the artists. Vellum stock was used to clearly communicate this duality.

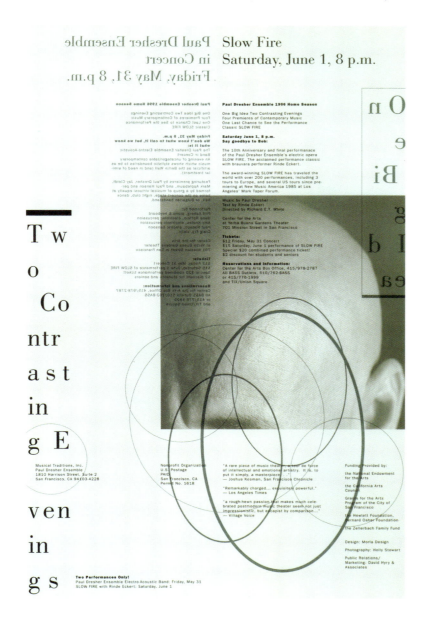

DESIGNERS Jennifer Morla, Craig Bailey   DESIGN FIRM Morla Design   CREATIVE DIRECTOR Jennifer Morla
CLIENT/PUBLISHER Paul Dresher   WRITERS David Hyry & Associates   PRINTER Vision Printing
PAPER Gilbert Gilclear   PHOTOGRAPHER Holly Stewart Photography   TYPOGRAPHER Morla Design

GREENHOOD+COMPANY

STATIONERY SYSTEM

ENTRANT'S COMMENTS   The stationery system for Greenhood+Company needed to be economical and flexible. This is a startup company, with the potential for major growth within the first year. Phone numbers, fax numbers, and e-mail addresses will probably change within a two-year period, so we designed the system using laser printing technology and rubber stamps. This was decided before we started the design so the "low-tech" production works with the design, not against it. The client's theme of "new media construction" was very inspirational and led to the choices in typography, layout, color, and paper. The solution is simple, progressive, yet has hints of the Russian constructivist style, an era of which our client is very fond.

DESIGNER Sam Lising   DESIGN FIRM Vrontikis Design Office   CREATIVE DIRECTOR Petrula Vrontikis

CLIENT/PUBLISHER Greenhood+Company   PRINTER Rubber stamp   PAPER Duratone Packing Carton, Construction Gold, Factory Green

HARLEY-DAVIDSON INC. 1995

ANNUAL REPORT

ENTRANT'S COMMENTS Harley-Davidson has initiated a plan that will provide the company with continuous improvement, competitive advantage, and relentless commitment to building top quality motorcycles. This year's report for Harley-Davidson focuses on this opportunity in terms of the company, the customers, and the shareholders. A collection of lifestyle photographs and detailed stories from all over the world begin to describe the passion and commitment of the Harley-Davidson experience. A collectible poster wraps the book and acts as a sleeve for the annual report.

DESIGNERS Curtis Schreiber, Ron Spohn   DESIGN FIRM VSA Partners, Inc.   ART DIRECTOR Dana Arnett

CLIENT/PUBLISHER Harley-Davidson Inc.   WRITER Ken Schmidt   PRINTER George Rice & Sons

PAPER Mead Escanaba, Mead Offset Enamel   PHOTOGRAPHER James Schnepf   TYPOGRAPHER VSA Parnters, Inc.

LIVING COLORS:
THE DEFINITIVE GUIDE TO COLOR PALETTES THROUGH THE AGES

BOOK

ENTRANT'S COMMENTS Apart from offering 80 color palettes from ancient to modern times, this book's double spiral binding serves a practical purpose and fulfilled a technical requirement. In order for the color palettes to be accurately reproduced, the color samples had to be printed separately from the text and illustration content. By using a double spiral binding, these separately printed components were combined in a easy to use, innovative format.

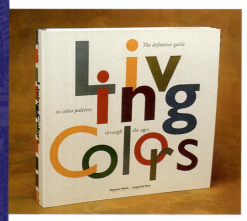

DESIGNER William Reuter   DESIGN FIRM Reuter Design   CREATIVE DIRECTOR Michael Carabetta   PUBLISHER Chronicle Books
AUTHORS Margaret Walch, Augustine Hope   PRODUCTION Nancy Reid, Julia Flagg   PRINTER Dai Nippon Press   PAPER 157 gsm. Gloss
PHOTOGRAPHERS Various   PHOTOGRAPHERS Reuter Design

MURAD 365 VITAMIN PACKAGING

PACKAGING

ENTRANT'S COMMENTS Murad 365 is a comprehensive line of personal care products that comes from a truly holistic approach—the notion that each day of the year is an opportunity to make the most of your beauty and health regimen by addressing your well being from within. The products range from skin and hair care to vitamins. The vitamin line, along with the 365 Spa Line, uses a symbol that represents the earth's 365-day orbit around the sun. The color palette breaks the vitamins into three groups: terra cotta for vitamins and minerals that come from the earth; green for herbal and plant derivatives; and gold for liquid supplements. From a production standpoint, the design team was adamant about using a recycled stock. Recycled envelope stock proved to be the perfect answer. It is extremely white and the finish is pleasantly smooth.

DESIGNERS Paul Farris, Catherine Cedillo, Mary Cay Walp   DESIGN FIRM Maddocks & Company   CREATIVE DIRECTOR Mary Scott

CLIENT/PUBLISHER Murad Inc.   PRINTER Spectrum (carton), Group One (labels)   PAPER Recycled envelope card stock

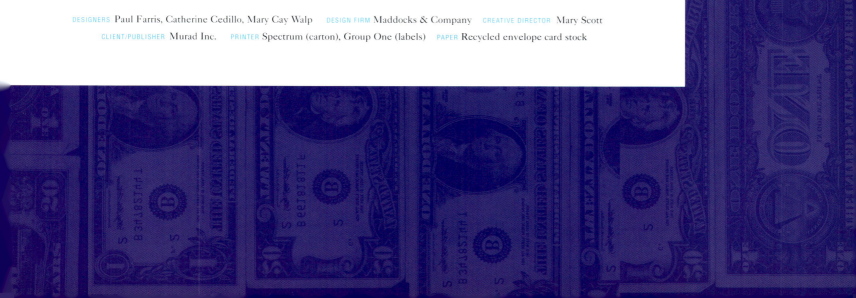

POETRY READINGS

POSTER

ENTRANT'S COMMENTS In seeking the quintessential image to express poetry, the metaphor of enlightenment assumes a separate dimension from the message.

DESIGNER Alexander Gelman   DESIGN FIRM Access Factory Inc.   CREATIVE DIRECTOR Alexander Gelman
CLIENT/PUBLISHER Biblio's   ILLUSTRATOR Alexander Gelman   PRINTER Mika   TYPOGRAPHER Alexander Gelman

WARREN-IDEA-EXCHANGE.COM

WEB SITE

ENTRANT'S COMMENTS Due to increased download time and the Web's low resolution, we decided against using intricate patterns and photographs in our design. Instead, we explored line art, because of its low expense, quick production time, and low image size. This also made our plans to animate the site through Shockwave and Java an easy and viable possibility. Images were created with only eight colors, and our seemingly large backgrounds were created with a mere ten pixels. The site complements our print work for S.D. Warren, but it has a life—and personality—all its own.

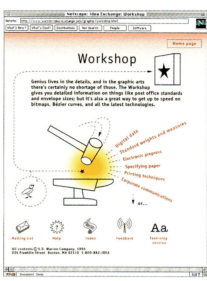

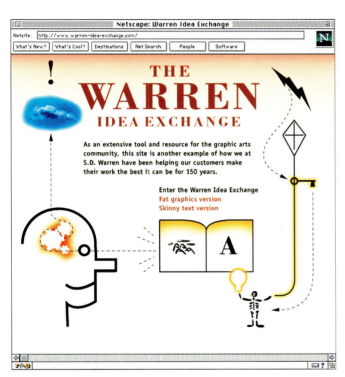

DESIGNER Alex Ku   DESIGN FIRM Siegel and Gale   CREATIVE DIRECTOR Cheryl Heller

DESIGN DIRECTOR Patrick O'Flaherty   CLIENT/PUBLISHER Corby Saunders, S. D. Warren   ILLUSTRATORS Barnes Tilney, Tony Hahn

SOFTWARE DESIGNERS Andrew Zolli, Kathleen Dolan, Tom Elia   PROJECT MANAGER Evan Orensten

THE TOPKAPI SCROLL
GEOMETRY AND ORNAMENT IN ISLAMIC ARCHITECTURE

BOOK

ENTRANT'S COMMENTS This, the inaugural title in the book series, "Sketchbooks & Albums", examines the Timurid pattern scroll in the collection of the Topkapi Palace Museum Library in Istanbul. The design strategy included using a horizontal format that echoes the scroll itself. The sense of linear flow was reinforced through the use of a consistent hang line for text and headers, and an asymmetric seven-column grid allowed for consistency and flexibility. The typeface, Minion, proved to resonate well with the geometric illustrations. The unity of these design parameters with the scroll, help to create an elegant and beautiful book.

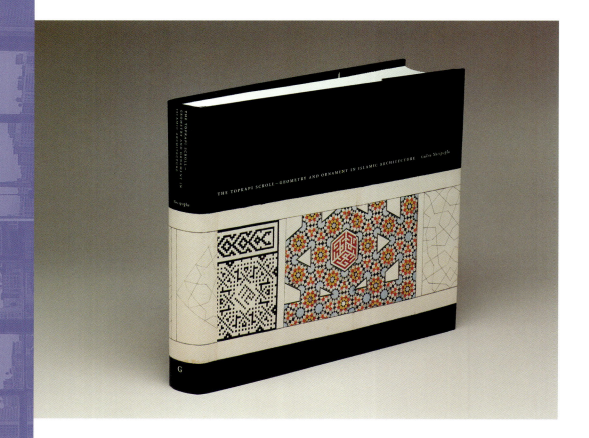

DESIGNER Simon Johnston   DESIGN FIRM Praxis Design   CREATIVE DIRECTOR Simon Johnston
CLIENT/PUBLISHER The Getty Center for the History of Art and the Humanities   AUTHOR Gülru Necipoglu   PRINTER The Stinehour Press
PAPER Monadnock Dulcet Neutral White   TYPOGRAPHER C & S Typesetters Inc.

SELECTED BY   ROBIN KINROSS   J. ABBOTT MILLER

THE TRUE HISTORY OF COCA-COLA IN MEXICO

POSTER

ENTRANT'S COMMENTS The poster, "The True History of Coca-Cola," is part of a continuing series for a local non-profit theater called "The Empty Space" to which NBBJ regularly donates design work. Each poster takes on a different character depending on donations of paper and printing, the play, and the designer involved. "Coca-Cola" is a fast-paced comedy featuring two actors who play dozens of characters with a bare minimum of crudely drawn scenery to set the stage. The poster reflects not only the low-budget, rowdy nature of the play, but the no-budget printing process as well. The imagery and most of the type are low-resolution scans blown up in the film process, and the printing was done on a web press on cheap newsprint, folded for that extra special offset touch. My main focus in the design process was (and still is) to avoid being sued by "the man."

DESIGNER Daniel R. Smith   DESIGN FIRM NBBJ Graphic Design   CLIENT/PUBLISHER The Empty Space Theater
PRINTER Pacific Publishing Co.   PAPER Newsprint   TYPOGRAPHER Daniel R. Smith

GSB REUNION 1996

MAP

ENTRANT'S COMMENTS How do you get a business school graduate interested in an under-attended alumni week-end? Appeal to the armchair traveler. Our invitation/map gives flight times, frequent flyer miles, airport information, and menu options for flights from alumni-inhabited cities to Chicago; alumni data for cities around the world; and time differences between each city and Chicago—in addition to listing all pertinent event data. Our client, a great collaborator, allowed us to invent the piece's content, and so we functioned as designer, author, and illustrator.

DESIGNERS Cheryl Towler Weese, JoEllen Kames   DESIGN FIRM studio blue   CREATIVE DIRECTORS Kathy Fredrickson, Cheryl Towler Weese   CLIENT/PUBLISHER University of Chicago, Graduate School of Business   WRITERS Kathy Fredrickson, Pat Nedeau   ILLUSTRATORS University of Chicago Map Room, studio blue   PRINTER Argus Press   PAPER Finch

VIZABILITY

INTERACTIVE CD-ROM

ENTRANT'S COMMENTS Based on a Stanford course by Bob McKim, VizAbility guides users through exploratory seeing, drawing, and diagramming exercises to enhance natural visual abilities. It encourages new ways of thinking, imagining, and communicating.

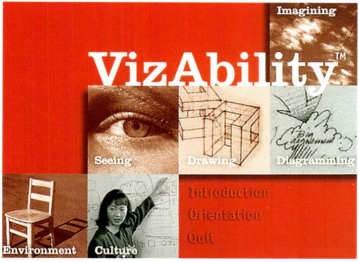

DESIGN FIRM MetaDesign   CREATIVE DIRECTOR Terry Irwin   CLIENT/PUBLISHER PWS Publishing   AUTHORS Kristina Hooper Woolsey, Scott Kim, Gayle Curtis   PROJECT DIRECTOR Jeff Zwerner   EXECUTIVE PRODUCERS Kristina Hooper Woolsey, Bill Hill   PRODUCER Bill Purdy   VIDEO EDITOR Don Ahrens   VIDEO PRODUCER Wendy Slick   PUZZLE DESIGNER Scott Kim   PROGRAMMER Marabeth Harding   WRITER Cindy Rink   ART PRODUCTION Jym Warhol

ROBIN KINROSS*

*DOWNPLAYING DESIGN "Meaning over look," "go for content." These were the watchwords I hoped would guide my selection of the Nineteenth Annual 100 Show. But the task wasn't a simple matter of choice and rejection according to clear criteria. At first, it seemed easier than I had expected. It was a matter of flagging pieces that looked interesting, and there was much that looked interesting. My abstract watchwords had some reality. For example, I tried to exclude designers' self-promotions and paper company brochures. But even some of these had interesting content. The truth was that we had been thrown into this huge pool of entries to inspect and sort, and we were swimming—trying to last the distance.

Though the judging takes place in the IBM Building's self-service cafeteria in Chicago, I felt that we were waiters attending to these artifacts laid out on the long tables. Certainly, over the two days of judging, we developed waiter's legs. Final selection became more difficult toward the end of the process. Our critical guards went up again. Some of the pieces that had become quite familiar to us now began to fade under renewed inspection and in the light of work that began to stand out as the most interesting.

Of course, the very idea of "meaning over look" is contradicted by the business of casting your eyes over a table full of leaflets or posters and fixing on those that look "most interesting." These are the ones whose look grabs you. But meaning fuels look, and the motto gathered some validation when, turning over a piece that drew me, I found that the designer had completed the section of the entry form that asked for comments on the job. (These forms are attached to the piece itself, usually on its reverse side.) Frequently, the pieces that looked most interesting were also the ones whose designers had taken the trouble to write comments here. Clearly, there was someone who had been involved with content, had cared about it, had been trying to do something with the job, especially under

SMALL TALK

INVITATION

ENTRANT'S COMMENTS

small talk.
small group.
small invite.
small type.
big success.

not talk focused on designers
but designers focused on talking.

no big deal.
just small talk.

great day, isn't it?

DESIGNERS Richard Cassis, Tracy West   DESIGN FIRM sparc   CREATIVE DIRECTOR Richard Cassis   CLIENT/PUBLISHER AIGA/Chicago

WRITER Richard Cassis   PRINTER ABS Graphics   PAPER MANUFACTURER S.D. Warren, Lustro Gloss Recycled

PHOTOGRAPHER Derek Snape   TYPOGRAPHER Richard Cassis, Tracy West

conditions of strict limitation.* At least for the designers of these pieces, there was meaning in the work. One booklet I turned over bore the comment "twenty-four-hour turnaround." It was a financial report with no obvious design features, only simple printing. I wanted to include it for what I imagined were the heroic conditions of its making. But in the end, it seemed just too undesigned to qualify.

Many of the pieces that stuck out on the grounds of "look" also stuck out for "meaning." Low-budget work such as "A True History of Coca-Cola", Artwalk, and Community AIDS Council posters carry their meaning in their look and feel, as well in their overt con-tent. All are minimal budget in appearance, though in different ways. "A True History of Coca-Cola" even looks as if it might have been created without a computer.

Among the pieces I noticed, there were several cultural-sector publications, with limited budget, which carried real content, giving the designer something to bite on. Then, the smallness of the budget often helped to sharpen the bite. For example, in the Gregory Markopolous catalog, two different papers are used (coated for pictures, uncoated for text) – a familiar though reward-ing way of organizing the content clearly, while perhaps cutting

ART OUT THERE

CATALOG

ENTRANT'S COMMENTS "Art Out There" documents interviews between public artists who were involved in a lecture series that took place at The School of the Art Institute of Chicago, plus an edited transcript of one of the lectures. I was interested in showing that the contents are more than Q and A sessions. The interviews are really discussions, and so I designed the catalog to reflect the exchange of thoughts and ideas between the artists.

DESIGNER Kali Nikitas   DESIGN FIRM graphic design for love (+ $)
CLIENT/PUBLISHER School of the Art Institute of Chicago   PRINTER Salsedo Press

costs at the same time. Here also, a twist is added by reusing color separations to make the pages that divide chapters. This is the terrain of the designer: to understand the content, and to shape the product and the production process so that this content is well taken-care-of and well-presented. Design done without designers tends – we would say – to miss something. But what exactly? And how does design differ from advertising? We chose some strong advertising work (Nike and Coca-Cola), which qualified because it seemed to show a "design" consciousness. But what is that? Some sense of restraint and overall coherence surely, both in formal means and in its tone (unlike the exaggeration that advertising traditionally uses). But beyond this, it's hard to specify.

I wanted to include information design, which I thought would provide good examples of my mottoes. But there was surprisingly little. The JBL EON Users Guide stands out almost on its own. There were a lot of pieces that borrowed from the mundane world of information – the undesigned sphere. Among the typical elements used were spiral binding, pastel colors (as in office copy paper), ruled paper, typewriter typefaces (notably Trixie), and an overall flirtation with drabness. The Boise Cascade Office Products annual report

ENTRANT'S COMMENTS This is a communication campaign to promote Artwalk, N.Y. , a day when artists in New York open their studios to walking tours. The proceeds benefit the Coalition for the Homeless. The objective was to introduce the concept to New Yorkers via posters, brochures and advertisements, and to explain how the tours work. The logo is very rough and derived from the "streets." This gritty logo is placed over a diffused rose, which is a traditional metaphor for beauty. The stark contrast between the juxtaposed images gives all of the communications its character.

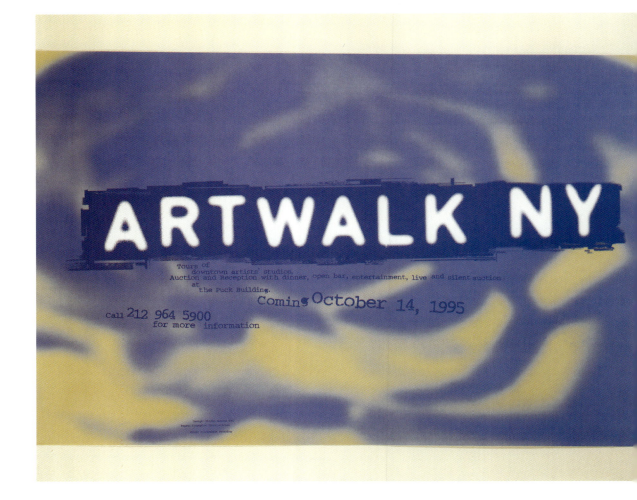

DESIGNERS Kaoru Sato, Jeffrey Morris   DESIGN FIRM Studio Morris
CREATIVE DIRECTOR Jeff Morris   CLIENT/PUBLISHER Coalition for the Homeless   PRINTER Innovation Printing
PAPER Champion, Carnival   PHOTOGRAPHER Doug Rosa

showed a good use of this "notebook aesthetic" (to coin a term} and justifiably, given the work of the company. These elements are also present in the Chicago Board of Trade annual report, the Chicago Volunteer Legal Services annual report, AIGA/Chicago Small Talk invitation, the RE:formations catalog, and Coca-Cola's A Brief on the Agency in Brief book.

One may see this appropriation of ordinariness as another attempt of design to get away from itself – another variation on the theme of the vernacular, which has run through twentieth-century architecture and design as a dialectical counterpart to the wish to

make it new. This desire to disappear into the background has always been present in modernism. It was there, for example, in Adolf Loos' love of English gentleman's tailoring and the perfectly-made and perfectly-discrete uniform; or in the Corbusian love of the typical, undesigned but satisfactory object (a pipe, a drinking glass). In this light, the post-modern interest in the vernacular – from Robert Venturi and Denise Scott Brown's championing of Las Vegas and forward – is simply a continuation of the modernist habit (but looking in another direction and out to offend). The same theme now returns in the work of essentially modernist architects,

CHICAGO VOLUNTEER LEGAL SERVICES

ANNUAL REPORT

ENTRANT'S COMMENTS At Chicago Volunteer Legal Services, lawyers work to protect the rights of people in the Chicago area who could not otherwise afford legal services. The annual captures the unique "do whatever it takes" spirit of the lawyers and the deep appreciation of the clients they serve.

DESIGNER Tim Bruce   DESIGN FIRM VSA Partners, Inc.   ART DIRECTOR Tim Bruce   DESIGN DIRECTOR Ted Stoik
CLIENT/PUBLISHER Chicago Volunteer Legal Services   WRITERS Margaret C. Benson, M. Lee Witte   PRINTER Bruce Offset
PAPER Mohawk Vellum   PHOTOGRAPHER Tony Armour   TYPOGRAPHER Tim Bruce

such as Herzog and De Meuron in Basel or Rem Koolhaas' OMA in Rotterdam, who enjoy banality, ordinariness, and the given.

It's clear that design can never get away from itself, however much it dreams of disappearing. Designer drabness is yet another ploy, but one that is refreshing in the present context in which high-gloss and perfect technique are easy and become ends in them-selves – a block to intelligent inquiry for both producers and users. As compared with high-gloss print production, which tends to smell unpleasant and to which readers' written annotations hardly adhere, the notebook aesthetic invites response from the user.

An uncoated and unvarnished surface, an informal layout that leaves free space, and a sense of itself as not yet complete – these are welcoming qualities in a print piece. Screen design is another issue, but one could make the same arguments for it concerning the pace of presentation, density of visual and auditory information, pro-vision of cues to the viewer, and so on.

So one comes back to the burden of design: to make sense and to find material form for this sense. Designers find different ways of doing this for different occasions at different times. There are agree-ments within the sphere of design: styles and approaches grow, coa-

GREGORY MARKOPOULOS

BOOK

ENTRANT'S COMMENTS The artist featured was one of the most influential avant-garde filmmakers of the 1950s and 1960s. The seductive and evocative imagery in the films had to be reflected in the plate section of the catalog, which was not meant to be overly designed. In the text section, the use of the blue-black color rather than process black and the manipulation of the images for the divider pages were meant to evoke the sense of mystery that marks his work.

DESIGNER Takaaki Matsumoto   DESIGN FIRM Matsumoto Incorporated   CREATIVE DIRECTOR Takaaki Matsumoto
CLIENT/PUBLISHER Whitney Museum of American Art   AUTHORS John Hanhardt, Matthew Yokobosky   PRINTER Herlin Press
PAPER Champion Kromekote, Simpson Starwhite Vicksburg, Tiara Smooth
PAPER PLATES Consolidated Reflections II   PHOTOGRAPHER Various   TYPOGRAPHER Takaaki Matsumoto

lesce, become imitated, grow moribund as the conditions that gave them life change, and perhaps are revived or reinvented in new guise. This is the culture of design, and it gives us a simple way of classifying products. Do they seem to belong to the culture of design? Are they made with that consciousness? No doubt it was this reflex judgment that led to our inclusion of Nike and Coca-Cola and to my exclusion of the twenty-four-hour turnaround brochure.

I hold to the idea that designed products look designed, not simply because they partake in the design culture but because there really is some *verzorging* in the process of their conception and production. Someone or some people really did care for meaning and sense. The artifacts we looked at on that judging weekend in Chicago suggest that this business of design is as difficult and interesting as it has ever been.

*This idea is well captured in the Dutch word *verzorgen*: to care for, which is applied to the design process as well as to, for example, looking after children. The "best-designed book" competition in the Netherlands is called *De Best Verzorgde Boeken*. In German-speaking countries, such competitions carry the title of the *Die Schönsten Bücher*: the most beautiful books.

SELECTED BY   ROBIN KINROSS

INSIGHT—MEDIA ART FROM THE MIDDLE OF EUROPE

EXHIBITION CATALOG

ENTRANT'S COMMENTS This exhibition was about video art from various countries in Central Europe. We borrowed from Bauhaus typographic influences but avoided the clichéd use of type and colors. Written by respected video artist Nina Czegledy, the type is featured boldly and prominently. The accompanying images vary greatly in quality and act as dividers for different sections of the catalog. The show, available on video, accompanies the catalog. Therefore, we sized it to fit a video cassette box.

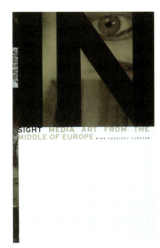

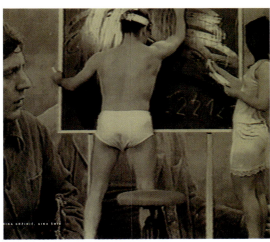

NINA GRŽINIČ, AINA ŠMID

MARINA GRŽINIČ

SPECIFIC STRATEGIES IN SLOVENE VIDEO ART PRODUCTION IN THE PRESENT POST-SOCIALIST PERIOD If we wish to reflect on the nineties in Ljubljana/Slovenia, we must first recall the eighties, the decade that left us a context and a reference and fatefully mapped our minds and bodies. The eighties created the most important concept of art and cultural life in Slovenia, and produced a new generation of (post)modern and (post)socialist painters, sculptors, photographers, fashion designers, video artists, etc., who produced an impressive number of art projects. Establishing a new style of visual "writing" in the nineties, which I intend to describe, involved a conscious visual reconfiguration of an "original" socialist and alternative cultural texture and structure, which resulted in innumerable "explosive" contrasts and a series of "technical imperfections" encompassing the outer and inner, sexual and mental, order and disorder, conceptual and political, original and recycled space and time. The eighties were witness to a renaissance of the video medium in Slovenia. This is not to suggest that we can speak about the birth of video art in the Yugoslavia of the seventies. Then, only the productions of Nuša and Srečo Dragan from Ljubljana and Sanja Iveković and Dalibor Martinis from Zagreb were known. There was no "Yugoslav" video, as such, only, as in the eighties, video productions that were the products of individual urban centres throughout the Yugoslav republics, that is, of Ljubljana, Zagreb, Belgrade, Skopje, and Sarajevo. The differences in production between these centres were acknowledged by Kathy Rae Huffman in her 1989 presentation at Artists' Space in New York, called "Deconstruction, Quotation, and Subversion." She referred to "video production from Yugoslavia," not Yugoslav video production. Thus the shift from the notion of "Yugoslav video" to "Slovene video," which has occurred almost overnight, does not require a difficult adjustment. Furthermore, in the eighties,

video production within Slovenia was so radically different aesthetically in comparison with local filmmaking and visual style that the designation "Slovene video production" could not in any way allude to the "national" unifying style which tried in the past almost obsessively to "colour" the cultural and social artefacts of a declined East Europe. The end of the seventies in Slovenia, commonly referred to as the end of authoritarian politics, marked a watershed for what had been until then an empty space in art. It was followed by the growth of a new youth "subculture" – punk. Punk culture and its artistic offshoots provided an uncompromising and critical energy which could evaluate and feed art creativity in the eighties, provoking shifts in the medium of art in general. It constituted and legitimated a space for new art production and granted a relevant status to diverse practices. It encouraged different socialization processes, new forms of social activity and behaviour, and the acceptance of "deviant" social and artistic "realities." During the eighties numerous new social movements were established in Slovenia, including the appearance of gay culture in Ljubljana. So, it is within the specific context of Ljubljana's new youth subculture during the eighties that the rebirth of the video medium and video art in Slovenia should be understood. Video in this context established itself quite quickly as an appropriate medium for the expression of the radical views of the new generation. The video productions of the eighties emerged primarily from the Students' Cultural and Art Centre (SKUC) and the Students' Cultural Forum Society (SKD Forum). In 1982 both of these centres together established a video section, which became the basis of SKUC-Forum independent video productions. Most of the first video works made by video artists and groups active through the eighties and today in the nineties (Marko Kovačič, Zemira Alaibegović and Neven Korda, former members of the multimedia group Borghesia, Marina Gržinić and Aina Šmid, etc.) were produced by SKUC-Forum. Nonprofessional video equipment (VHS), with its simple handling, and extremely fast production and reproduction – which allowed the repeated performance of new messages – made video one of the most popular and radical forms of media for the eighties generation. Access to video became a status symbol in itself. As the new medium in Slovenia, the full boundaries of video are yet to

DESIGNERS Diti Katona, Susan McIntee   DESIGN FIRM Concrete Design Communciations Inc. (Toronto)   CLIENT/PUBLISHER XYZ Artists' Outlet   WRITER Nina Czegledy   PRINTER C. J. Graphics   PAPER EuroDull   PHOTOGRAPHER Various   TYPOGRAPHER Concrete Design Communications Inc.   ART DIRECTORS Diti Katona, John Pylypczak

JOHANNES VERMEER

EXHIBITION CATALOG

ENTRANT'S COMMENTS The design focused on paintings in the exhibition. Each catalog entry was an even number of pages; if the text and accompanying photos ran to an odd number, a detail was included. Reproductions of the remaining Vermeer works, which were not included in the exhibition, were interspersed throughout the four essays. These illustrations were smaller than those of the exhibition paintings, but were located higher than the majority of the black-and-white comparative figures, giving them prominence. The book was published in Dutch, German, Italian, and French. The wide top margin was included to provide room for languages with a greater word count.

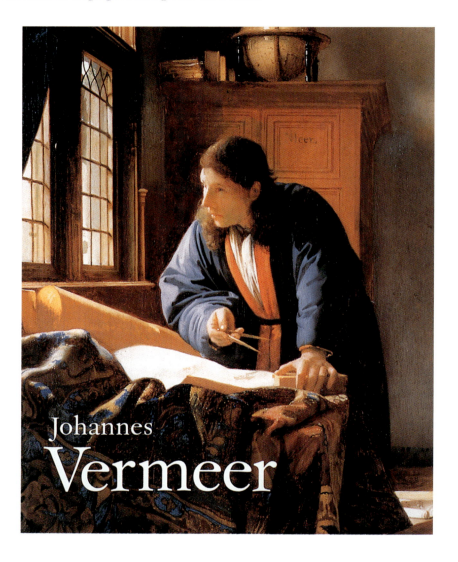

DESIGNER Chris Vogel   DESIGN FIRM National Gallery of Art

CREATIVE DIRECTOR Frances Smyth   CLIENT/PUBLISHER National Gallery of Art   WRITER Arthur K. Wheelock, Jr.

PAPER Waanders, Mc Scheufelen   PHOTOGRAPHERS Various   TYPOGRAPHER General Type

KING LEAR AND THE SKRIKER

POSTERS

ENTRANT'S COMMENTS The Public Theater posters are individual components of an overall identity (visual language) which I designed for the institution. The fall season uses the cacophony of Victorian wood typefaces which are emblematic of the theater. "The Skriker" poster promotes an individual play about a demon, with the wood type absorbed into the demon. "King Lear" features F. Murray Abraham in the title role. In the poster, the wood type becomes Lear's crown.

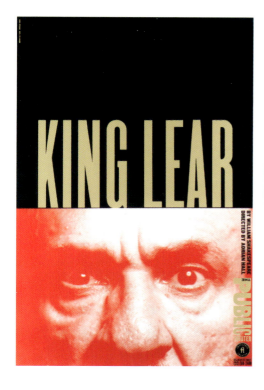

DESIGNERS Paula Scher, Lisa Mazur   DESIGN FIRM Pentagram Design   CREATIVE DIRECTOR Paula Scher
CLIENT/PUBLISHER The Public Theater   PHOTOGRAPHER Peter Harrison (King Lear only)

new avatar. The future potential of what can be "me" goes far beyond today's simple cursor. We now have unlimited options for designing representations of ourselves – and then using those representations to interact with others.

Microsoft Chat and *The Palace* illustrate the extremes of consistent design language versus personal expression. This dichotomy represents another design challenge. *Microsoft Chat* works well because it employs a design language that is consistent with its metaphor. A breakthrough will come when Microsoft extends the design language to the user level, allowing the users to design "me" from a language of elements and behaviors that accrete to become the avatar. In this scenario, an interaction designer will not design avatars, instead creating the specialized tools through which users design avatars for specific interface genres.

Getting tools into the hands of average users will mean that increasingly our work as designers will be meta-design or, as John Rheinfrank describes it, designing the proto-objects, the clay with which others do their own design. Those of us who have design training will be designing ways for others to design for themselves.

SEEING OUR WORK

Advances in networked media change the way we see our work by shifting the boundaries within which we *do what we do*. (Note that I did not write: *do our work*.) Consider the transformation of the desktop interface. This innovation is called *Net-top* by Netscape and "true web integration" by Microsoft. Whatever the name, both of these browsers are at the heart of the transformation.

Microsoft's *Explorer* 4.0 provides seamless navigation between the desktop and everything out there on the Web. Why is this single *Explorer*-based view an important innovation? It means that boundaries between where you are – in your computer files, in your company Intranet, or out on the net at large – become blurred. From a user's perspective, this is fantastic. Imagine a person writing a paper using *Microsoft Word*. He constantly reflects on his notes, then shifts to other articles and sites on the web. Today, these are all different *places* that require different types of interaction, even though the writer tends to see everything as part of the same paper-writing activity.

With a single *Explorer*-based view, the different places become more alike and more seamlessly integrated with the underlying activity. This makes work easier. The *Explorer* 4.0 active desktop allows for more control over the interface, enabling the elimination or addition of components. People can design more of their desktop world (as any HTML page) to suit their specific needs and not feel forced into the one-size-fits-all interface of an operating system.

There is a down-side, however. Some people may get confused about where they are, on their machine or out on the Net. The browser is probably not the right interface for all activities. The *Explorer* 4.0 view is not really a window onto the world of the Web, it is a simulation of the world coming to the desktop. Microsoft's biggest accomplishment (apart from the fact that *Explorer* 4.0 is a nice-looking interface) is providing that simulation. The interface suggests the kind of seamlessness in activity that enables people to move smoothly through it.

There are many interfaces that are better than browsers for interacting with complex networks of information[5]. If this is the onset of the next generation of operating interfaces, we should be worried. *Explorer* 4.0 technology ties everything even more deeply into features of *Windows* 95, such as the *TaskBar* and *Start* menu. But it is still the same old windows, icons, menus, etc., interaction devices originated by Xerox in the '70s. Holding on to the desktop as the driving metaphor, Microsoft places the workplace and its instrumental value (*Word*, *Excel*, etc.) at the heart of interaction.

COLD WATER

The qualities of *MSNBC*, *Microsoft Chat*, and *Explorer* 4.0 described above suggest that Microsoft is beginning to understand the power of good design. In fact, no company is better positioned to dominate the field completely. As good as Microsoft's designers have shown themselves to be, we need them to push the limits even more. They need to be willing to pursue a more fundamental exploration of the interface experience. The trio of examples taken together provide a glimpse of what it could be like to provide users with what they really want – support for activities like living, learning, playing, and working with experiential value. This is the promise of embedded networked media; computing integrated with what we do, like the quality of cold integrated into ice water.

[1] Originally meaning 'an artificial device to replace missing parts of the body,' this has come to mean an artificial addition or supplement to the five senses, something that extends human capabilities. Linda Stone, *Microsoft Vision*, April 14, 1997

[2] See *Design Languages in Bringing Design to Software* by Terry Winograd, Addison-Wesley 1996

[3] E. Brethenoux, Gartner Group www.gartner.com

[4] Microsoft claims to be working on a Microsoft Chat character creation kit, which would allow users to create their own avatars.

[5] *Bye-Bye, Browser - Hello, OS* by Chris Oakes http://www.wired.com/news/technology/story/2800.html

THE [ECO]LOGIC OF MATERIALIZATION AND DEMATERIALIZATION

SUZETTE SHERMAN AND PETER STATHIS

This is not the first time we have been asked to co-author an essay, but it is the first occasion to work as collaborators in selecting products and citing them for a meritorious position in an annual review. We both began our survey independently, but with the shared intent of assessing the recent product landscape through important contemporary trends. In spite of our personal relationship of fifteen years and the similarity within our separate surveys, we each selected very distinct products. What surprised us was the sheer divergence of our selections, portraying to us the radical differences in how we each view the near future.

Yet we both attempted to find answers to the same riddle: how the 'natural' and the 'artificial' could negotiate a mutual future in a kind of 'techno[eco]logical' object culture – a culture sustained by a design process centered around an extensive consideration of the complex relationships between industrial production, its resultant products, and their effect on the environment. The traditional framework of viewing 'artificial' and 'natural' as dissimilar entities has been rendered useless. We must now acknowledge that we exist in a 'neo-natural' superindustrialized society; one that has pushed the environmental consequences of its industrialization to extremes.

Individually, our answer came in product examples that endorse bipolar ideologies, best characterized as 'materialization' and 'dematerialization'. Within this 'techno[eco]logical' framework, materialization is an attempt to come to grips with our advanced system of production and consumption, particularly within the design of recyclable products, the reuse of materials, and the use of recycled materials in production. Dematerialization, on the other hand, represents an inverse approach. It can be understood as a type of source reduction effecting a decline over time in the real weight or actual energy expended in the production and consumption of consumer goods, or as a more broad economic function conceptualizing an ecology of artifacts (or product environment) rather than a single object.

Even if these two visions represent oppositional strategies toward our built environment, we came to the conclusion that they are wholly symbiotic. The pervasive notion that we are experiencing a shift from a culture that produces hard material goods to one that produces (and ultimately rewards) soft immaterial goods is only partly true. French social scientist Abraham Moles maintains that any immaterial society will be heavily materialized because its immaterial products are necessarily linked to a deep mechanical infrastructure that creates and manages them, suggesting the ecological need to highlight our link between energy and lifestyles. The hard material goods our postmodern society makes still matter, now more than ever, given our rising techno[eco]logical condition. How we make them matters most. Annual design journals chronicle how design objects have evolved, but they also show how the nature of the design system has not – so far.

MATERIALIZATION

SUZETTE SHERMAN

In society's recent efforts to maximize the general efficiency of our material usage and consider its cradle-to-grave impact on what Buckminster Fuller would call "Spaceship Earth," we have developed a wide range of considerations for the design process to optimize overall production efficiency and protect our finite and closed ecological system. I term these considerations 'design attributes,' the most commonly recognized of these being recycling. Currently, we all come in contact each day with more (recycled) eco-materialization than one would suspect. Recycling has achieved a strong foothold in packaging, having infiltrated beneath layers of glossy print. Yet it is still in its infancy, particularly in relation to the consumer products this packaging houses. Widespread recycling beyond packaging is all but undetectable. As its field of technological research matures, our palette of new (recycled) materials will grow correspondingly, resulting in a variety of remarkably reclaimed surfaces surrounding us in more conspicuous forms.

Most designers view secondary materials as unsightly, and unworthy of use as an appearance surface of a product. Yet, as products with confident designs that dispel this traditional rationale become commercially available and widespread, consumers will embrace these 'new/old' materials, much as we accepted the sudden appearance of plastic fifty years ago. Through innovation and commitment, recycled materials cannot only live up to today's technical and aesthetic standards of manufacturers, designers, and consumers, but also promise higher levels of standards altogether.

Philippe Starck's *Jim Nature* television, manufactured by Thomson Consumer Electronics under the brand name *Saba*, is not hot off the production line, but its relatively recent introduction is significant. I believe fifty years from now design researchers will look back at this particular design as representing that moment in history when high-design embraced low-tech (reclaimed materials) in a way that ultimately led the way to important cultural innovations in the product landscape. Currently, there are several other mass-produced, design-sensitive products that also utilize secondary materials, such as Herman Miller's *Aeron* chair and Knoll's *Parachute* chair, but neither have allowed the integrity of the recycled content to honestly "face the public."

While radical in appearance, what is unique about Starck's television is not actually a technological innovation, but an updating of an out-of-favor process dating back to the 1940s. The sawdust outer shell is a molded composite of recovered wood shavings added to a phenolic (plastic) resin base, much like Bakelite or Kys-ite. Traditionally, Bakelite uses recovered sawdust (wood flour); Kys-ite (no longer produced) added recycled newspaper pulp to the mix. The introduction of these crude plastics was followed by refinement and ultimate mass acceptance. Updated material continues the evolution of this long standing recycling-based process, and ultimately a refinement of this material will become mainstreamed as well.

What distinguishes *Jim Nature* from similar products of the past is its size (much larger), its typology (extended beyond ashtrays and appliance knobs), and appearance (unapologetically celebrating its reclaimed status). By simply amplifying the scale and quantity of particulate matter, *Jim Nature* provides a radical new aesthetic to consumers, allowing them to signal to others their own particular set of values embodied in that aesthetic. Starck illustrates how the banal can be transformed to a higher ecological order.

A recent evolution of environmentally-sensitive molded composites is used in the *Rothko* chair designed by Alberto Lievore and manufactured in Spain by Inert. For such a spare design, the innovations are numerous. This chair is produced from a material called *Maderón* (Spanish for a large piece of wood) which incorporates a byproduct of almond processing. The almond flour resulting from ground shells can be considered a (neo)natural resource for Spain, whose almond industry is the second largest in the world and produces 300,000 short tons of discarded shells annually. Much like Starck's television, the quantity of particulate matter is loudly pronounced within the resin base, giving the indication of a fine, light colored, solid wood product. Again, the technological advances here are in the product's size, typology, and surface appearance.

The *Rothko* chair's unique structural properties are assisted by a wire frame armature embedded within its Maderón skin. Suddenly, properties never before achievable are made possible. Maderón allows the postmodern production of products, typically cost-prohibitive in more natural woods, to become relatively inexpensive to produce and readily available to many. The artificial nature evidenced in the *Rothko* chair indicates how far we have come in our conceptual framework regarding natural order and technological advance. I believe we are merely beginning a long and optimistic design journey.

DEMATERIALIZATION

PETER STATHIS

These two projects exemplify what is possible in consumer goods when designers break free of both time-worn use scenarios and the traditional paradigmatic constraints of product. What emerges are two techno[eco]logical proposals whose object qualities go far beyond their material constitution. They conceptualize products with [hyper]formance qualities such as brightness, thinness, lightness, and flexibility intended to be used in a multi-sensory participatory process that is externalized, extensive, customizable, and relaxed.

As lifestyles move towards a synthesis of mechanical production and electronic reproduction, these products acknowledge that we are now at the fault line where actual materiality and virtual immateriality collide.

Virtual Vision Computer Cap, designed by Vent Design Associates, is the first and

only commercially available, hands-free, roaming, head mounted, digital viewing display computer system with speech recognition and audio feedback. The *Computer Cap* contains a patented monocular display offering a resolution where graphics as precise as medical x-rays, digitized maps, and intricate diagrams can be viewed clearly while the wearer/viewer is either stationary or in motion. The see-through optic display becomes transparent to the wearer/viewer when not in use and does not need to be removed in order to re-enter and interact within a "non-augmented" reality.

All of the literally hundreds of pounds of technology that would more than fill an entire desktop is miniaturized and uniquely mounted to an ergonomic cap, humbly inspired by both baseball players and long-distance truckers. The *Computer Cap* can be used for the most demanding applications, from a navigational GPS boating system to instantaneous medical record retrieval. Unrestricted use of the hands gives freedom of movement in surgery, or wherever access to information and concurrent activity must be seamless.

The *Computer Cap* is constructed of a featherweight, easily fabricated, die-cut closed-cell Neopren/Lycra jersey material. The electronic housings are an injection molded short-carbon fiber and thermoplastic polyester blend, resulting in the most minimum of armatures. The *Cap* is designed for easy access and repair, and the entire product's electronics are interchangeable and upgradable, promoting not only a light, but long, product life.

Techtoo™: *Software and Hardware as Temporary Tattoos and High Performance Jewelry* is an experimental project by Summer Powell and Melissa Paul of Cranbrook Academy of Art. Their proposal suggests that in these postmodern times, a longing for tribal association and cultural identity is more vital now than ever. *Techtoo*™ engages

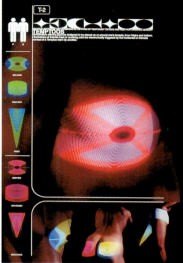

the archetypal role of tattoos and other forms of jewelry by utilizing these rituals as a social rite of passage or as a means to realize a more authentic self. Yet it understands that today's world of fleeting images and mutant materials calls for an appearance as ephemeral as these times embody. If a tattoo traditionally signaled an allegiance forever, then a *Techtoo*™ is for a moment, offering augmented realities and synthetic pleasures.

The metaphor of temporary tattoos as software and advanced jewelry as hardware, designates the interface between one's self and another. It suggests how dozens of PDA's and other personal electronic products can be rendered immaterial. The body has been turned inside-out, positioning the skin as the surface where cultural codes are transformed via temporary products that inscribe the flesh with new sensory experience.

Techtoos™ are categorized to comprise five sensory scenarios.

Tunetoos. Tribal audio emblems, pre-tuned to digital satellite frequencies, are directly applied onto a flexible antenna. Advanced jewelry takes the form of headphone/speakers, powered by a solar storage array, allowing for private listening or shared localized play.

Temptoos. Temperature altering patches are placed on or around one's breasts, inner thighs, and bottom. Sensations of intense heat or numbing cold are electronically triggered by the incidental or intimate contact of a *Temptoo*™ worn by another.

Scentoos. Scent packets embedded with micro-fragrance cells are designed to be placed over one's erogenous zones. Odor is electronically emitted and its intensity controlled at will by applying contact to a corresponding "skin-switch," in effect "closing the circuit" and triggering its release.

Chemtoos. Digital strips worn about the face, head, and back carry natural stimulants and smart drugs. Their release can be programmed by an encoded microchip clock to insure delivery at the appropriate moment.

™*toos.* Body as billboard, a neo-tribal marking for the postmodern kindred. One's self-image changes as the *Techtoo*™ identity immaterially changes with the coming of each fashion season.

SOFT HARDWARE
AND HARD MATERIAL

MICHAEL McCOY

The most interesting products from 1996 show me the way toward a softer vocabulary of form and materials in hardware and experimentation with *smart materials* – materials that respond dynamically to changing conditions and forces. Smart products that are simpler and cheaper than personal computers and that are dispersed around our working and living environments must fit more naturally and comfortably into our lives and routines. I am beginning to see some products and concepts appear that fit nicely.

The *eMATE 300* from Apple Computer is a portable computer designed specifically for the rigors of the educational environment. Essentially a *Newton* with a keyboard, the *eMATE's* organically shaped, rugged, green tinted translucent plastic housing protects it in a situation which, for a computer at least, is fraught with peril. It suits the school culture, its interpretive community.

The shape is much more robust than typical laptops and affords generous surfaces to grasp. It also provides a surface for students to rest their arms while drawing on the screen with the stylus which fits into an inkwell on the side. As information and communication devices become tailored to their cultural contexts, we should see more adventuresome product form languages that speak eloquently to specific audiences. The *eMATE* is one of the first of this new breed of products.

The *Cable Turtle* is a very clever soft product solution to a problem that once would have been resolved by separate mechanical parts bolted together. Comprised of a rubber shell, which is flopped open to receive the excess wires from today's plethora of personal electronics (telephone, television, etc.), the *Turtle* snaps closed to secure and conceal excess wires. From the sneer of the lips around the cable exit to its soft, yo-yo quality, it is a wonderful, witty solution to an

everyday problem with an added bit of sensuality and humor. Even opening and closing it is engaging. (I found myself absent-mindedly playing with one on my desk while I was on the phone.) Such a human and witty solution to one of the everyday, prosaic problems of life seems to be what design is all about.

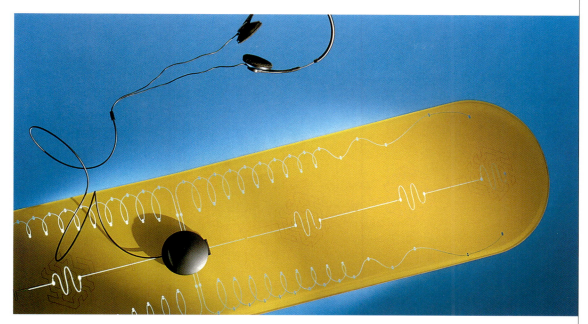

The *Biofeedback Snowboard* by Don Carr is an example of a product constructed with a so-called smart material. It is made of composite material that responds to body motions and gestures with sonic energy. Embedded in the snowboard are electronic pressure sensing devices that interpret the forces created as one swoops down the slopes, carving turns and catching air. The board turns those forces into harmonic sounds that are played back into earphones worn by the snowboarder. The effect is simultaneous motion and music. A form of bio-feedback, the 'boarder is aware of both the physical motion and the sonic response. The visible circuitry reveals the sensitive and responsive nature of the board. The *Biofeedback Snowboard* is in the vanguard of new smart products that sense changing conditions and mutate their physical or electronic form in response.

The *D.O.C.* (dockably open computer) by Cristiano Nogueira, a student at the Institute of Design at Illinois Institute of Technology, shows what can happen to the form of technology when the designer thinks carefully about the user's daily routine. The computer takes the form of docks that are linked like the cars in a train. The elements of the computer, each uniquely shaped, can be dropped into any dock. Designed especially for people who need to transport components, such as hard drives or modems, among different work locations, the modules are easily recognizable and can be slipped quickly into a pocket or backpack on the way out the door. Its playful, toy-like quality fits the domestic context and is a welcome relief to electronic devices that seem to be more at home in the office.

Another student project, *Bound Packet Computing* by Gary Natsume at Cranbrook Academy of Art, proposes computer components as soft pages that clip into a binder (similar to a three ring binder) to comprise a highly customizable laptop computer. There are five pages (or packets), a screen, keypad, motherboard, drive, and battery that clip into a connective spine to create a fully functional computer. Additional spaces for more components easily accommodate upgrades. The binder cover can be made from a number of materials including leather or fabric, allowing the owner to customize it. The soft materials make it more inviting to curl up with in your favorite easy chair than the rigid plastic boxes of current laptops.

The trend toward soft hardware and smart materials reflects a movement away from the fixed mechanical assemblages of the industrial age and toward more subtle methods for solving everyday problems. Designers begin to look at solutions that are comfortable with the body, the home, and living. It is the ultimate convergence of the industrial age and the electronic age; the merging of mechanical and informational operations into one intelligent and responsive composition.

DESIGN FIRMS

ACCESS FACTORY INC.
New York, NY

AFTER HOURS CREATIVE
Phoenix, AZ

AGNEW MOYER SMITH
Pittsburgh, PA

ANTENNA
Indianapolis, IN

THE APOLLO PROGRAM
Greenwich, CT

ATLANTIC RECORDS
New York, NY

BJ KRIVANEK ART + DESIGN
Chicago, IL

BIELENBERG DESIGN
Boulder, CO

ANDREW BLAUVELT
Minneapolis, MN

BRUCE MAU DESIGN INC.
Toronto, Ontario, Canada

CAHAN & ASSOCIATES
San Francisco, CA

CHRONICLE BOOKS
San Francisco, CA

CONCRETE DESIGN
COMMUNICATIONS INC.
Toronto, Ontario, Canada

CRANBROOK ACADEMY OF ART
Bloomfield Hills, MI

D IS FOR DESIGN
Royal Oak, MI

DAVID CARSON DESIGN
San Diego, CA

DRENTTEL DOYLE PARTNERS
New York, NY

DUFFY DESIGN
Minneapolis, MN

EMIGRE
Sacramento, CA

FITCH, INC.
Worthington, OH

FRANKFURT BALKIND PARTNERS
New York, NY

FROETER DESIGN CO.
Chicago, IL

NAN GOGGIN, KAREN COLE
University of Illinois
Champaign, IL

GRAPHIC DESIGN FOR LOVE (+ $)
Chicago, IL

RENATE GOKI
Urbana, IL

IRS RECORD CO.
Culver City, CA

INDUSTRIAL STRENGTH DESIGN
New York, NY

JAGER DIPAOLO KEMP DESIGN
Burlington, VT

LEIMER CROSS DESIGN CORP.
Seattle, WA

MYV NETWORKS
New York, NY

MADDOCKS & COMPANY
Los Angeles, CA

MARK RAKATANSKY STUDIO
Ames, IA

MARSUPIAL
New York, NY

MATSUMOTO INCORPORATED
New York, NY

META4DESIGN
San Francisco, CA

MODERN DOG
Seattle, WA

MOFLA DESIGN
San Francisco, CA

NBBJ GRAPHIC DESIGN
Seattle, WA

NATIONAL GALLERY OF ART
Washington, DC

KATHLEEN OGINSKI/
GREG VAN ALSTYNE
New York, NY

PAM CERIO DESIGN
Cleveland, OH

PENTAGRAM DESIGN
New York, NY

PETRICK DESIGN
Chicago, IL

PLUS DESIGN INC.
Boston, MA

PRAXIS DESIGN
Pacific Palisades, CA

REY INTERNATIONAL
Los Angeles, CA

RECORDING INDUSTRY
ASSOCIATION OF AMERICA
Washington, DC

MOLLY RENDA
Durham, NC

JOHN ROUSSEAU, DESIGNER
Birmingham, MI

SAGMEISTER INC.
New York, NY

SIEGEL AND GALE
New York, NY

SOS, LOS ANGELES
Los Angeles, CA

SPARC
Chicago, IL

STOLTZE DESIGN
Boston, MA

STUDIO BLUE
Chicago, IL

STUDIO MORRIS
New York, NY

THORBURN DESIGN
Minneapolis, MN

TOLLESON DESIGN
San Francisco, CA

MARTIN VENEZKY
San Francisco, CA

VSA PARTNERS, INC.
Chicago, IL

VERVE RECORDS
New York, NY

VISUAL DIALOGUE
Boston, MA

VRONTIKIS DESIGN OFFICE
Los Angeles, CA

WAGES DESIGN
Atlanta, GA

WALKER ART CENTER
Minneapolis, MN

WARNER BROS. RECORDS
Burbank, CA

WERNER DESIGN WERKS INC.
Minneapolis, MN

WIEDEN & KENNEDY
Portland, OR

ANDREA WOLLENSAK,
KLAUS KEMPENAARS
New London, CT

MICHAEL WORTHINGTON
Los Angeles, CA

CONTRIBUTORS

SHELLEY EVENSON'S groundbreaking practice in interaction design focuses on the iterative process of envisionment and embodiment. Clients include Apple Computer, Hewlett Packard, Emerson Electric, NCR, Philips, Sun Microsystems, and Xerox. She has presented at several ACD Living Surfaces conferences, conducted ACM/SIGCHI workshops, and developed the original design for ACM's interaction magazine. Currently, she is the Nierenberg Chair of Design at Carnegie Mellon University.

SOMI KIM is a graphic designer living and working in Los Angeles, a city whose complexities provoke and inspire her work as a partner in the studio *ReVerb*. She is a graduate advisor for new media projects at Art Center College of Design and has lectured extensively. Recipient of a 1995 Chrysler Award for Innovation in Design, *ReVerb* encourages a collective strategy that often utilizes different collaborations, both within the group and with other studios.

ROBIN KINROSS is a typographer, writer, and publisher based in London and Amsterdam. He started the imprint *Hyphen Press* in 1980, while teaching at the University of Reading (England), to re-publish Norman Potter's book *What is A Designer*. The list now includes works by Dutch type designer Fred Smeijers and Swiss book designer Jost Hochuli, as well as his own book *Modern Typography* and his pamphlet *Fellow Readers*. As a writer, he has long associations with *Information Design Journal*, *Blueprint*, and *Eye*.

MICHAEL McCOY is a senior lecturer at the Institute of Design of Illinois Institute of Technology, and a partner of both McCoy & McCoy and Fahnstrom/McCoy of Chicago, Illinois. His industrial design practice includes furniture and the design of high technology products for Knoll International, NEC, ACCO, and Steelcase. He has received the European Ergodesign Award, IDSA's IDEA Award, and the Chrysler Award for Innovation in Design.

J. ABBOTT MILLER is a designer, writer, curator, and educator whose projects are concerned with with the cultural and educational role of design. His many notable exhibitions and publications include *The Process of Elimination: The Bathroom, The Kitchen and the Aesthetics of Waste*, (done in collaboration with Ellen Lupton); *Printed Letters: The Natural History of Typography*; and *Dance Ink Magazine*. His writing has been published extensively and has served as the editor of the American Center for Design's magazine *Statements*. In 1994, he was awarded - with Lupton - the first annual Chrysler Award for Innovation in Design.

MICHAEL ROCK is a designer and writer. Together with Susan Sellers and Georgianna Stout he is a partner in 2x4, a studio in New York City, and he is also an associate professor of Design at the Yale School of Art. In addition, he is a contributing editor and design critic for *I.D.* magazine. His writings have appeared in publications including *I.D.*, *Eye*, *Print*, *Design Issues*, *AIGA Journal*, and others.

SUZETTE SHERMAN is an environmental journalist and researcher of the principles and practices of environmentally sound design. She has worked with the Environmental Defense Fund, the American Institute of Graphic Arts, the Industrial Designers Society of America, and the Package Design Council on issues concerning design's impact on the environment. She co-curated the exhibition "Garbage Out Front" at the New York Municipal Art Society.

PETER STATHIS is head of the 3D Department and Designer-in-Residence at Cranbrook Academy of Art, Bloomfield Hills, Michigan. He is founder of Virtual Studio, which develops technoculturally advanced products, furniture and lighting. His work has been published and exhibited internationally, including the Museum of Modern Art's recent 'Mutant Materials' exhibition, and has been selected for the design collections of several U.S. museums.

PRODUCTION

PAGE COMPOSITION A template of the design was created on the master pages of a QuarkXPress 3.32 document. Text provided in a word processing format was imported into the document and low resolution versions of the images were placed for position.

IMAGES Image of the winning entries and for the essays were provided as low resolution images for placement, cropping and sizing. The pictures for the "frames" consisted mostly of snapshots and three-dimensional original art that was scanned at low resolution. Other images were downloaded from the Web.

FILM INPUT The images were scanned on Crosfields 656M and 636E. The QuarkXPress files were opened on a Power Mac 8100. Page make up was done on the Mac by replacing the positional low-resolution images with color-corrected high-resolution images.

FILM OUTPUT High resolution post-script files were then sent to the Scitex Dolev 450 for final film output at 175 linescreen using Kodak films and Kodak processing chemistry.

PROOFING Machine-pressed proofs were created on a Dainippon KF-124-GL on European matte art paper and using Japanese Morohoshi ink.

PRINTING The book was printed inline on a Heidelberg Speedmaster 102 using Fuji printing plates and solvent-based four-color process inks. The cover was gloss laminated. The book text was printed on Nymolla Matt Paper 150gsm. The cover was printed on Nymolla Artpaper 135 gsm.

BINDING The book was thread-sewn in 16 page signatures, separate endpapers, square-backed, fully cased with head and tail bands and jacketed.

COLOPHON

BOOK DESIGN   Aline Ozkan, Michael Rock
              2x4, New York

PRODUCTION   Provision Pte Ltd, Singapore
              Tel: +65 334 7720
              Fax: +65 334 7721

SOFTWARE   QuarkXPress, Adobe Photoshop

FONTS   Helvetica, Caslon 540